POEMS
FOR A GOOD
AND HAPPY
LIFE

POEMS
FOR A GOOD
AND HAPPY
LIFE

Compiled and with Introductions
by Myrna Reid Grant

DOUBLEDAY DIRECT LARGE PRINT EDITON

CrossAmerica
BOOKS

This Large Print Edition, prepared especially for Doubleday Direct, Inc., contains the complete unabridged text of the original Publisher's Edition.

Designed by Randall Mize
Printed in the United States of America

ISBN 0-7394-0237-4

Published by CrossAmerica™ Books, an imprint of Crossings Book Club,
Box GB, 401 Franklin Avenue, Garden City, New York 11530.

CrossAmerica™ Books trademark registration pending on behalf of Crossings Book Club

Unless otherwise noted, Scripture quotations are from the New Revised Standard Version.

For acknowledgments, please see p. 407

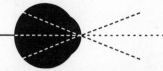

This Large Print Book carries the
Seal of Approval of N.A.V.H.

In memory of my mother,
Florence Grace Jackson Reid

CONTENTS

JUSTICE

COURAGE

MODERATION

HOPE

LOVE

xvi

xvii

INTRODUCTION

EVERYONE WANTS to be happy and to have a good life. Experts say personal happiness depends on getting a good start in life, on what opportunities a person is given, on education, personal faith, health, or marrying the right person. Yet people who have had many advantages still can be uncertain about how a happy and moral life can be lived out in a culture where there are so many differing opinions on what's right and what's wrong.

America grew to become a great nation because it was founded on a consensus of religious convictions and values. Those traditions no longer shape the lives of large numbers of Americans. A moral vacuum has been unintentionally created by courts of law, boards of education, and public institutions by their sincere efforts to respect and give voice to the differing viewpoints of groups and individuals. One of the results of this moral vacuum is that American students are educated without learning ethical guidelines. Some schools have tried to encourage students to construct their own principles by consulting their feelings about right and wrong, but this tactic has dismally failed these students when faced with the complexity of "the real world."

At the heart of today's school reform movement is the conviction that children need to be *taught* moral reasoning. The current Character Education Movement, with its stress on *respect and responsibility;* the Association for Moral Education; the Points of Light Foundation; the "Enough is Enough" campaign; the Institute on Religion and Democracy; Students Taking a Right Stand, and many other organizations and campaigns offer a variety of theories on the requisite values and ethical principles for guiding America into the twenty-first century.

The ancient world believed in the concept

of virtue. The Greek philosophers defined virtue as "essential attitudes and habits." They named four supreme virtues necessary for happiness and the good life that human beings are capable of practicing. These virtues are called "cardinal" from a Latin word that means "hinge" because all other virtues hang on them. Christian thinkers, beginning in the fourth century, added three more indispensable virtues to this group, bringing the total number of the cardinal virtues to seven. The conviction that these timeless virtues lead to happy and good lives has held strong for more than fifteen hundred years, and the ancient virtues continue to have profound relevance for us today. In their simplicity and grandeur, they rise above modern cultural debates and religious, political, and national divisions.

Poems for a Good and Happy Life is divided into seven sections, one for each virtue. The old English words for the seven cardinal virtues are *prudence, justice, fortitude, temperance, faith, hope, and charity.* In the passing of centuries, the meanings of some of these words have changed. This book, therefore, uses modern names for four of these virtues: *wisdom* for prudence; *courage* for fortitude; *moderation* for temperance; and *love* for charity. The first four virtues—wisdom, justice, courage, and moderation—are called the *natural virtues* because the Greeks, from Socrates to Plato and Aristotle, maintained that ordinary people have the natural human capacity to attain these qualities if they have the desire and discipline to do so. Aristotle taught that the way people acquire virtue is by repeatedly practicing the virtues so that they eventually become second nature.

The last three virtues, faith, hope and love, arise out of the late Roman and medieval Christian worlds. They are called the *supernatural virtues* because people can't just *try* to have them. The church fathers explained that these virtues are special gifts given by God through Christ. After receiving them the believer then puts the gifts into action. Ambrose, Augustine, and particularly Thomas Aquinas regarded all seven cardinal virtues as absolutely central to the Christian life and as a summary of the highest moral teachings of the Church.

Throughout the centuries, Jewish tradition and classical literature, including the

Scriptures, also contributed to humankind's understanding of virtue, ethics, and morality. Particular Jewish norms and expressions of morality reflect the *universal* values and the responsibilities of one human person or society to another. Judaism's vast teachings on wisdom, justice, courage, family, community, and responsibility enrich our modern understanding of the issues and concepts associated with the cardinal virtues.

Poets, however, do not ordinarily create poems by means of logic or theology. Their art emerges from the way they see the world, from their feelings and from the connections they make with reality. Poetry can cause us to think, and it also can startle and delight us, making us feel deeply.

Putting this book together gave me months of pleasure. To spend so much time with great poets of the past and present, to listen to their voices, to see the world through their eyes, to think their thoughts, has been a labor of love. I learned it is important to read poetry very slowly, or better, to read it aloud; I lost much of any poem if I read it only once or quickly. As I worked, I was often touched by the realization that the hopes, dreams, griefs, joys, loves, and ambiguities I discover in myself as I live in our rushed, postmodern, technological age are the very same inner worlds described by poets in earlier centuries and "simpler times." By the time I came to the end of this project, I had gained a renewed and deep respect for the art of the poet and the greatness of the human spirit reflected in so many of the poems.

I am honored to have among my friends some of the poets whose work appears in this book. I give them heartfelt thanks for sharing their work with me. I owe special thanks to my daughter, Jennifer, herself a poet and writer, whose creativity, suggestions, and insights made this a better book. Many of my friends and students suggested poems and gave encouragement, and I thank each one. I am grateful to Paul Snezek, colleague and friend, to my graduate assistant, Ann Guthormsen, and to Pat Wright, secretary, for their invaluable technical assistance. Thanks to editors at Crossings for their encouragement and for their vision for the book. To my family, who have given so much loving support, lifelong thanks are due. Extra appreciation goes to the littlest family members, my grandchildren, for themselves, each one, being a poem.

MYRNA GRANT
Wheaton, Illinois
August 1996

POEMS
FOR A GOOD
AND HAPPY
LIFE

WISDOM

THE BOOK OF PSALMS says, "The price of wisdom is above rubies." Proverbs also counsels, "Wisdom is the principal thing: therefore get wisdom." The ancient word for wisdom as a cardinal virtue is *prudence*. What the word "prudence" meant long ago is very different from what prudence has come to mean today. In our world, to be prudent is to be cautious in the handling of one's affairs. This understanding of the world can suggest a lack of courage, and even a compromise of integrity in the service of practicality and common sense. Often, it's not a compliment to be called a prudent person.

The words "practical wisdom" give a

better idea of what the Greeks meant by *prudence.* They explained that wisdom is the ability to see what is at stake and to know how rightly to respond. Today we assume that people learn from experience. We say that "experience is the best teacher" and it makes us wise. We recognize, however, that only *some* people learn by experience. Others make the same mistakes over and over again. Why is experience a teacher only for some individuals?

Thomas Aquinas, the great Christian theologian and philosopher, wrote a famous book, *Treatise on the Virtues,* in which he explored the ways that people develop the skills to make good and wise decisions. First, he said, individuals must do all that they can to reconstruct past experiences realistically. This initial step is the most slippery one (as any psychologist knows), because a person's memories can be selective. For various reasons, people tend to remember only negative past experiences, or only the good. In addition, people are prone to falsify memory, to subtly shift the truth or omit painful aspects of reality, to alter perceptions in their own favor. To counter these very human tendencies of memory, an individual must first decide to look honestly at the past.

The second step toward wisdom is to be open-minded. Wisdom can't be gained by people who are inflexible and have already made up their minds. Seeking the mature viewpoints and opinions of others contributes to one's own understanding. Aquinas gently observes that it is possible to act well not only as a result of one's own good deliberation but also by taking the advice of a wise person.

Thirdly, the person who is seeking wisdom has to rise above the emotions of past experiences and think rationally and objectively. One may be able to recall past experiences without bias, be willing to change a perception, and yet be gripped with emotion as one recalls the past. To achieve practical wisdom, one has to be humble enough to give up the desire to justify one's past actions or ideas. Aquinas said that when these three processes are worked through, the mind is free to make good judgments.

The Greeks exalted wisdom. Of the four ancient cardinal virtues, wisdom was the supreme virtue, above courage, justice, and moderation. So fundamental is this virtue that the Greeks said an individual couldn't even possess the other three virtues without first attaining wisdom. They reasoned that people could not be *courageous* if they didn't first know the reality of a danger and the implications of their action. People could not be *just* if they hadn't wisely considered a specific situation before making a judgment. People couldn't live lives of balance and *moderation* if they couldn't be realistic, open-minded, and objective about themselves.

Christian theology affirms the ancient instructions on wisdom, and recognizes a clear spiritual dimension to the virtue. Scripture teaches that wisdom is an attribute of God, revealed not only in the world of nature, but also in redemption. The wise individual accepts both reason and divine revelation. The church fathers verified the Greek teachings about the primary importance of right and moral decisions, but they stressed that life's judgments are to be made not only for living in this world but also for life in the world to come.

The poems of wisdom that follow teach, advise, and observe life's foibles and ambiguities. Many give insights into wisdom that are all the more striking because of their subtlety. Christina Rossetti's small poem, "What Are Heavy?" captures profound wisdom within its few lines.

What Are Heavy?

What are heavy? sea-sand and sorrow:
What are brief? today and tomorrow:
What are frail? Spring blossoms and
　youth:
What are deep? The ocean and truth.

　—CHRISTINA ROSSETTI

A Baby-Sermon

The lightning and thunder
They go and they come;
But the stars and the stillness
Are always at home.

—GEORGE MacDONALD

Untitled

This poem is taken from the words supposedly spoken by the Queen of Sheba before a long journey to Jerusalem to visit King Solomon, famous for his wisdom. Her visit is recorded in I Kings, chapter 10.

Wisdom is
sweeter than honey,
brings more joy
than wine,
illumines
more than the sun,
is more precious
than jewels.
She causes
the ears to hear
and the heart to comprehend.

I love her
like a mother,
and she embraces me
as her own child.

I will follow
her footprints
and she will not cast me away.

—MAKEDA, QUEEN OF SHEBA

The Rainy Day

The day is cold, and dark, and dreary;
It rains, and the wind is never weary;
The vine still clings to the moldering wall,
But at every gust the dead leaves fall,
    And the day is dark and dreary.

My life is cold, and dark, and dreary;
It rains, and the wind is never weary;
My thoughts still cling to the moldering
    Past,
But the hopes of youth fall thick in the
    blast,
    And the days are dark and dreary.

Be still, sad heart! and cease repining;
Behind the clouds is the sun still shining;
Thy fate is the common fate of all,
Into each life some rain must fall,
    Some days must be dark and dreary.

—HENRY WADSWORTH LONGFELLOW

The Cat

Lessons in life often can be learned by observing the behavior of animal friends.

Observe the Cat upon this page.
Philosophers in every age,
The very *wisest* of the wise
Have tried her mind to analyze
In vain, for nothing can they learn.
She baffles them at every turn
Like Mister Hamlet in the play.
She leads their reasoning astray;
She feigns an interest in string
Or yarn or any rolling thing.
Unlike the Dog, she does not care
With common Man her thoughts to share.
She teaches us that in life's walk
'T is better to let others talk,
And listen while *they* say instead
The foolish things *we* might have said.

—OLIVER HERFORD

(The Robin Is the One)

The Robin is the One
That interrupts the Morn
With hurried—few—express Reports
When March is scarcely on—

The Robin is the One
That overflows the Noon
With her cherubic quantity—
An April but begun—

The Robin is the One
That speechless from her Nest
Submit that Home—and Certainty
And Sanctity, are best

—EMILY DICKINSON

A Rule

Do all the good you can,
By all the means you can,
In all the ways you can,
In all the places you can,
At all the times you can,
To all the people you can,
As long as ever you can.

—JOHN WESLEY

Wisdom in the Book of Proverbs

Happy are those who find wisdom, and
those who get understanding,
for her income is better than silver, and her
revenue better than gold.
She is more precious than jewels, and nothing you desire can compare with her.
Long life is her right hand; in her left hand
are riches and honor.
Her ways are ways of pleasantness, and all
her paths are peace.
She is a tree of life to those who lay hold of
her; those who hold her fast are called
happy.

—Proverbs 3:13–18

Do not forsake her, and she will keep you; love her, and she will guard you.

The beginning of wisdom is this: Get wisdom, and whatever else you get, get insight.

Prize her highly, and she will exalt you; she will honor you if you embrace her.

She will place on your head a fair garland; she will bestow on you a beautiful crown.

—Proverbs 4:6–9

The fear of the Lord is the beginning of wisdom, and the knowledge of the Holy One is insight.

—Proverbs 9:10

Against Idleness and Mischief

How doth the little busy bee
Improve each shining hour,
And gather honey all the day
From every opening flower!

How skillfully she builds her cell!
How neat she spreads the wax!
And labors hard to store it well
With the sweet food she makes.

In works of labor or of skill,
I would be busy too;
For Satan finds some mischief still
For idle hands to do.

In books, or work, or healthful play,
Let my first years be passed,
That I may give for every day
Some good account at last.

—ISAAC WATTS

To-day

Children of Carlyle's Victorian era were taught to use time productively.

So here hath been dawning
Another blue day;
Think, wilt thou let it
Slip useless away?

Out of Eternity
This new day is born;
Into Eternity,
At night will return.

Behold it aforetime
No eye ever did;
So soon it for ever
From all eyes is hid.

Here hath been dawning
Another blue day;
Think, wilt thou let it
Slip useless away?

—Thomas Carlyle

17

Whole Duty of Children

A child should always say what's true
And speak when he is spoken to,
And behave mannerly at table;
At least as far as he is able.

—ROBERT LOUIS STEVENSON

Polonius's Advice to His Son

Give thy thoughts no tongue,
Nor any unproportion'd thought his act.
Be thou familiar, but by no means vulgar.
Those friends thou hast, and their
  adoption tried,
Grapple them to thy soul with hoops of
  steel;
But do not dull thy palm[1] with
  entertainment
Of each new-hatch'd, unfledg'd[2] courage[3].
Beware
Of entrance to a quarrel, but, being in,
Bear't that th' opposed may beware of
  thee.
Give every man thy ear, but few thy voice;
Take each man's censure[4], but reserve thy
  judgment.
Costly thy habit as thy purse can buy,
But not express'd in fancy; rich not gaudy;
For the apparel oft proclaims the man;

[1] Too freely shake hands
[2] Untested
[3] A young man of spirit
[4] Disapproval

Neither a borrower, nor a lender be;
For loan oft loses both itself and friend,
And borrowing dulls the edge of
   husbandry[5].
This above all—to thine own self be true,
And it must follow, as the night the day,
Thou canst not then be false to any man.

—WILLIAM SHAKESPEARE, *Hamlet,* Act I,
   Scene 3

[5] Careful management of resources

Speech to the Young
Speech to the Progress-Toward
(Among them Nora and Henry III)

Say to them
say to the down-keepers,
the sun-slappers,
the self-soilers,
the harmony-hushers,
"Even if you are not ready for day
it cannot always be night."
You will be right.
For that is the hard home-run.
Live not for battles won.
Live not for-the-end-of-the-song.
Live in the along.

—GWENDOLYN BROOKS

Eternity

Blake shares his wisdom that life's joys are fleeting and are best held in an open hand.

He who binds to himself a joy
Does the winged life destroy
But he who kisses the joy as it flies
Lives in eternity's sun rise.

—WILLIAM BLAKE

Jacob

Perhaps Garrett takes the idea for his poem from the Old Testament story (Genesis 32:24) of Jacob wrestling with the angel.

Years and scars later
I finally learn
all angels travel
under assumed names

—GEORGE GARRETT

Virtue

Sweet day, so cool, so calm, so bright,
The bridal of the earth and sky;
The dew shall weep thy fall to night,
   For thou must die.

Sweet rose, whose hue angry and brave
Bids the rash gazer wipe his eye;
Thy root is ever in its grave,
   And thou must die.

Sweet spring, full of sweet days and
 roses,
A box where sweets compacted lie;
My music shows ye have your closes,
   And all must die.

Only a sweet and virtuous soul,
Like seasoned timber, never gives;
But though the whole world turn to coal,
   Then chiefly lives.

—GEORGE HERBERT

Leisure

In this age of electronic amusements and rushed schedules, our lives are greatly enriched when we make time to enjoy the beauty of the natural world.

What is this life if, full of care,
We have no time to stop and stare.

No time to stand beneath the boughs
And stare as long as sheep or cows.

No time to see, when woods we pass,
Where squirrels hide their nuts in grass.

No time to see, in broad daylight,
Streams full of stars, like skies at night.

No time to turn at Beauty's glance,
And watch her feet, how they can dance.

No time to wait till her mouth can
Enrich that smile her eyes began.

A poor life this, if, full of care,
We have no time to stand and stare.

—W. H. DAVIES

(Tell All the Truth But Tell It Slant)

Often it is wise to tell the truth gently and gradually so that people are able to receive it.

Tell all the Truth but tell it slant—
Success in Circuit lies
Too bright for our infirm Delight
The Truth's superb surprise

As Lightning to the Children eased
With explanation kind
The Truth must dazzle gradually
Or every man be blind—

—EMILY DICKINSON

Lose the Day Loitering

Lose the day loitering, twill be the same
  story
Tomorrow, and the next more dilatory[1],
For indecision brings its own delays,
And days are lost lamenting o'er lost days.
Are you in earnest? Seize this very minute!
What you can do, or think, you can, begin
  it!
Only engage, and then the mind grows
  heated;
Begin it, and the work will be completed.

—JOHANN WOLFGANG VON GOETHE

[1] Intending to delay

Stopping by Woods on a Snowy Evening

Pleasure can distract us from our goals and commitments.

Whose woods these are I think I know.
His house is in the village though;
He will not see me stopping here
To watch his woods fill up with snow.

My little horse must think it queer
To stop without a farmhouse near
Between the woods and frozen lake
The darkest evening of the year.

He gives his harness bells a shake
To ask if there is some mistake.
The only other sound's the sweep
Of easy wind and downy flake.

The woods are lovely, dark and deep,
But I have promises to keep,
And miles to go before I sleep,
And miles to go before I sleep.

—ROBERT FROST

There Is a Beauty at the Goal of Life

There is a beauty at the goal of life,
A beauty growing since the world began,
Through every age and race, through
    lapse and strife
Till the great human soul complete her
    span.
Beneath the waves of storm that lash and
    burn,
The currents of blind passion that appall,
To listen and keep watch till we discern
The tide of sovereign truth that guides it
    all;
So to address our spirits to the height,
So attune them to the valiant whole,
That the great light be clearer for our light,
And the great soul the stronger for our
    soul:
To have done this is to have lived, though
    fame
Remember us with no familiar name.

—ARCHIBALD LAMPMAN

29

The Red Wheelbarrow

One of the most significant components of wisdom is the ability to truly see. The poet remarks that much depends on this.

so much depends
upon

a red wheel
barrow

glazed with rain
water

beside the white
chickens.

—WILLIAM CARLOS WILLIAMS

First Memory

The poet's childhood anger against her father actually revealed how much she had loved him.

Long ago, I was wounded. I lived
to revenge myself
against my father; not
for what he was—
for what I was: from the beginning of time,
in childhood, I thought
that pain meant
I was not loved.
It meant I loved.

—Louise Glück

What the Butcher Knows

There are many skills and much knowledge the butcher employs that, metaphorically, people could make good use of in life.

How to dismember,
how to separate the fat,
how the muscles stick to the bone
how to detach wings
how to loosen joints
how to smack pink coils into a paper
    boat.

Every morning he puts on a
freshly starched apron
and unsheathes his knife from the carving
    block,
he walks through the freezer jostling
sides of beef, setting them moving like
impatient children standing on one
foot and then the other.

He knows about the insides of things,
tucking the neck into the hollow chicken,
stuffing sausages into translucent socks.

Probably he also knows
what to do with feathers,
brains, hooves.

Wrapping packages of prim chops,
he sees beyond today.
He knows how things turn out if they
are not snatched up.

   —JILL PELÁEZ BAUMGAERTNER

Light Within

He that has light within his own clear
   breast
May sit i' the center, and enjoy bright day:
But he that hides a dark soul and foul
   thoughts
Benighted walks under the midday sun;
Himself his own dungeon.

   —JOHN MILTON

Miracles

Why, who makes much of a miracle?
As to me I know of nothing else but
  miracles,
Whether I walk the streets of Manhattan,
Or dart my sight over the roofs of houses
  toward the sky,
Or wade with naked feet along the beach
  just in the edge
  of the water,
Or stand under the trees in the woods,
Or talk by day with any one I love, or
  sleep in the bed at
   night with anyone I love,
Or sit at table at dinner with the rest,
Or look at strangers opposite me riding in
  the car,
Or watch honey-bees busy around the
  hive of a summer forenoon,
Or animals feeding in the fields,
Or birds, or the wonderfulness of insects
  in the air,
Or the wonderfulness of the sundown, or
  of stars shining so quiet and bright,
Or the exquisite delicate thin curve of the
  new moon in spring;

These with the rest, one and all, to me are
  miracles,
The whole referring, yet each distinct and
  in its place.

To me every hour of light and dark is a
  miracle,
Every cubic inch of space is a miracle,
Every square yard of the surface of the
  earth is spread with the same,
Every foot of the interior swarms with the
  same.

To me the sea is a continual miracle,
The fishes that swim—the rocks—the
  motion of the waves—the ships with
  men in them,
What stranger miracles are there?

—WALT WHITMAN

The Waking

Roethke was awarded a Pulitzer Prize in 1954 for his book of poems titled, The Waking.

I wake to sleep, and take my waking slow.
I feel my fate in what I cannot fear.
I learn by going where I have to go.

We think by feeling. What is there to
  know?
I hear my being dance from ear to ear.
I wake to sleep, and take my waking slow.

Of those so close beside me, which are
  you?
God bless the Ground! I shall walk softly
  there,
And learn by going where I have to go.

Light takes the Tree; but who can tell us
  how?
The lowly worm climbs up a winding stair;
I wake to sleep, and take my waking slow.

Great Nature has another thing to do
To you and me; so take the lively air,
And, lovely, learn by going where to go.

This shaking keeps me steady. I should
  know.
What falls away is always. And is near.
I wake to sleep, and take my waking slow.
I learn by going where I have to go.

—THEODORE ROETHKE

Auguries[1] of Innocence

To see a World in a Grain of Sand
And a Heaven in a Wild Flower
Hold Infinity in the palm of your hand
And Eternity in an hour
A Robin Red breast in a Cage
Puts all Heaven in a Rage
A dove-house filld with doves & Pigeons
Shudders Hell thro all its regions
A dog starvd at his Masters Gate
Predicts the ruin of the State
A Horse misusd upon the Road
Calls to Heaven for Human blood
Each outcry of the hunted Hare
A fibre from the Brain does tear
A Skylark wounded in the wing
A Cherubim does cease to sing
The Game Cock clipd & armd for fight
Does the Rising Sun affright
Every Wolfs & Lions howl
Raises from Hell a Human Soul
The wild Deer, wandring here & there
Keeps the Human Soul from Care
The Lamb misusd breeds Public strife

[1] Signs

And yet forgives the Butchers Knife
The Bat that flits at close of Eve
Has left the Brain that wont Believe
The Owl that calls upon the Night
Speaks the Unbelievers fright
He who shall hurt the little Wren
Shall never be belovd by Men
He who the Ox to wrath has movd
Shall never be by Woman lovd
The wanton Boy that kills the Fly
Shall feel the Spiders enmity
He who torments the Chafer's sprite
Weaves a Bower in endless Night.
The Catterpiller on the Leaf
Repeats to thee thy Mothers grief
Kill not the Moth nor Butterfly
For the Last Judgment draweth nigh
He who shall train the Horse to War
Shall never pass the Polar Bar
The Beggars Dog & Widows Cat
Feed them & thou wilt grow fat
The Gnat that sings his Summers song
Poison gets from Slanders tongue
The poison of the Snake & Newt
Is the sweat of Envys Foot
The Poison of the Honey Bee
Is the Artists Jealousy
The Princes Robes & Beggars Rags

Are Toadstools on the Misers Bags
A truth thats told with bad intent
Beats all the Lies you can invent
It is right it should be so
Man was made for Joy & Woe
And when this we rightly know
Thro the World we safely go
Joy & Woe are woven fine
A Clothing for the soul divine
Under every grief & pine
Runs a joy with silken twine
The Babe is more than swaddling Bands
Throughout all these Human Lands
Tools were made & Born were hands
Every Farmer Understands
Every Tear from Every Eye
Becomes a Babe in Eternity
This is caught by Females bright
And returnd to its own delight
The Bleat the Bark Bellow & Roar
Are Waves that Beat on Heavens Shore
The Babe that weeps the Rod beneath
Writes Revenge in realms of death
The Beggars Rags, fluttering in Air
Does to Rags the Heavens tear
The Soldier armd with Sword & Gun
Palsied strikes the Summers Sun
The poor Mans Farthing is worth more

Than all the Gold on Africs shore
One Mite wrung from the Labrers hands
Shall buy & sell the Misers Lands
Or if protected from on high
Does that whole Nation sell & buy
He who mocks the Infants Faith
Shall be mockd in Age & Death
He who shall teach the Child to Doubt
The rotting Grave shall neer get out
He who respects the Infants faith
Triumphs over Hell and Death
The Childs Toys and the Old Mans
   Reasons
Are the Fruits of the Two seasons
The Questioner who sits so sly
Shall never know how to Reply
He who replies to words of doubt
Doth put the Light of Knowledge out
The Strongest Poison ever known
Came from Caesars Laurel Crown
Nought can deform the Human Race
Like to the Armours iron brace
When Gold & Gems adorn the Plow
To Peaceful Arts shall Envy Bow
A Riddle or the Crickets Cry
Is to Doubt a fit Reply
The Emmets Inch & Eagles Mile
Make Lame Philosophy to smile

He who Doubts from what he sees
Will neer Believe do what you Please
If the Sun & Moon should Doubt
Theyd immediately Go out
To be in a Passion you Good may do
But no Good if a Passion is in you
The Whore & Gambler by the State
Licencd build that Nations Fate
The Harlots cry from Street to Street
Shall weave Old Englands winding Sheet
The Winners Shout the Losers Curse
Dance before dead Englands Hearse
Every Night & every Morn
Some to Misery are Born
Every Morn & every Night
Some are Born to sweet delight
Some are Born to sweet delight
Some are Born to Endless Night
We are led to Believe a Lie
When we see not Thro the Eye
Which was Born in a Night to perish in a
   Night
When the Soul Slept in Beams of Light
God Appears & God is Light
To those poor Souls who dwell in Night
But does a Human Form Display
To those who Dwell in Realms of day

  —WILLIAM BLAKE

What Is the World?

This is a piece too fair
To be the child of Chance, and not of
    Care.
No Atoms casually together hurl'd
Could e'er produce so beautiful a world.

—JOHN DRYDEN

Fortune

There is a tide in the affairs of men
Which, taken at the flood, leads on to
fortune;
Omitted, all the voyage of their life
Is bound in shallows and in miseries.
On such a full sea are we now afloat,
And we must take the current when it
serves,
Or lose our ventures.

—WILLIAM SHAKESPEARE,
Julius Caesar, Act 4, Scene 3

Mending Wall

*Some people live by following old slogans
without questioning their wisdom. The speaker
in this poem challenges his neighbor's catch-
phrase, "Good fences make good neighbors."*

Something there is that doesn't love a
    wall,
That sends the frozen-ground-swell under
    it,
And spills the upper boulders in the sun;
And makes gaps even two can pass
    abreast.
The work of hunters is another thing:
I have come after them and made repair
Where they have left not one stone on a
    stone,
But they would have the rabbit out of
    hiding,
To please the yelping dogs. The gaps I
    mean,
No one has seen them made or heard
    them made,
But at spring mending-time we find them
    there.
I let my neighbor know beyond the hill;

And on a day we meet to walk the line
And set the wall between us once again.
We keep the wall between us as we go.
To each the boulders that have fallen to
 each.
And some are loaves and some so nearly
 balls
We have to use a spell to make them
 balance:
"Stay where you are until our backs are
 turned!"
We wear our fingers rough with handling
 them.
Oh, just another kind of out-door game,
One on a side. It comes to little more:
There where it is we do not need the wall:
He is all pine and I am apple orchard.
My apple trees will never get across
And eat the cones under his pines. I tell
 him.
He only says, "Good fences make good
 neighbors."
Spring is the mischief in me, and I wonder
If I could put a notion in his head:
"Why do they make good neighbors? Isn't
 it
Where there are cows? But here there are
 no cows.

Before I built a wall I'd ask to know
What I was walling in and walling out,
And to whom I was like to give offence.
Something there is that doesn't love a
  wall,
That wants it down." I could say, "Elves"
  to him,
But it's not elves exactly, and I'd rather
He said it for himself. I see him there
Bringing a stone grasped firmly by the top
In each hand, like an old-stone savage
  armed.
He moves in darkness as it seems to me,
Not of woods only and the shade of trees.
He will not go beyond his father's saying,
And he likes having thought of it so well
He says again, "Good fences make good
  neighbors."

—ROBERT FROST

The Wheel

for Malcolm Muggeridge

I stepped down from the train,
saw you there, old man, bent
next to the tudor station, smiling
and waving to me over the steering wheel.
Your aged blue eyes
saw us through the maze of roads

walled by high corn and close trees, roads
which branch away from the train
station to the cottage, to your wife's eyes
and worn wrinkled skin. Her back bent
over the low table. You turn the wheel
and press the horn, she's smiling,

face tilted up to the window. I smiled
as we chose sticks to sturdy our walk on
    dirt roads
that circle your farm . . . the windmill's
    wheel
spinning in the moving air, the train's
cry; muted by distance and wind-bent
corn. Shaded by silk, its small yellow
    eyes.

I could see in your eyes
the smiling
knowledge that your days are bent
around time, its roads
winding and short, brief as the call of the
    train,
disappearing with the double-drum beat of
    its wheels.

A bird perched on the tractor wheel
its tiny black eyes
alert and trained
to see the smiling
orange cat. Wings spread over the road
In beating flight. I'm bent

on being like you in age, bent
on sitting visitors beside the wheel,
driving them to strawberry sandwiches
    and my roads
to support their journey. Meeting eyes.
I wish to be smiling
as I collect them at the train.

Your brows are bent now, and in your
   eyes
images spin like a wheel. You're smiling
out at the roads, not hearing the cry of the
   train.

—Jennifer Grant

It's Unbecoming

It's unbecoming to have fame
For this is not what elevates,
And there's no need to keep archives
Or dote over your manuscripts;

Creation's way is—to give all,
And not to bluster or eclipse:
How mean, when you don't signify,
To be on everybody's lips!

But life must be without pretense;
Conduct your days that finally
You may indraw far-distant love
And hear the call of years to be.

And gaps you leave must not be found
Amid your papers, but in fate:
A whole life's chapters, and contents
You may correct or annotate.

Plunge then into obscurity,
Concealing it in every pace
Just as the landscape disappears
Into the fog, and leaves no trace.

For others on the living trail
Will step by step pursue your way,
Yet you yourself must not discern
What is defeat, what victory:

And never for a single instant
Betray your true self, or pretend,
But be alive, and only living,
And only living, to the end.

　　—BORIS PASTERNAK,
　　　translated by Henry Kamen

What Endures

Nothing endures but personal qualities.

What do you think endures?
Do you think a great city endures?
Or a teeming manufacturing state? or a
prepared constitution? or the best built
steamships?
Or hotels of granite and iron? or any
chef-d'oeuvres[1] of engineering, forts,
armaments?

Away! these are not to be cherish'd for
themselves,
They fill their hour, the dancers dance, the
musicians play for them,
The show passes, all does well enough of
course,
All does very well till one flash of defiance.

[1] Masterpieces

A great city is that which has the greatest
men and women,
If it be a few ragged huts it is still the
greatest city in the whole world.

—WALT WHITMAN

And Yet the Books

And yet the books will be there on the
    shelves, separate beings,
That appeared once, still wet
As shining chestnuts under a tree in
    autumn,
And, touched, coddled, began to live
In spite of fires on the horizon, castles
    blown up,
Tribes on the march, planets in motion.
"We are," they said, even as their pages
Were being torn out, or a buzzing flame
Licked away their letters. So much more
    durable
Than we are, whose frail warmth
Cooled down with memory, disperses,
    perishes.
I imagine the earth when I am no more:
Nothing happens, no loss, it's still a
    strange pageant,
Women's dresses, dewy lilacs, a song in
    the valley.

Yet the books will be there on the shelves,
  well born,
Derived from people, but also from
  radiance, heights.

—Czeslaw Milosz

Tree at My Window

*Nature often has insights to give us about our-
selves, if we pay attention.*

Tree at my window, window tree,
My sash[1] is lowered when night comes
   on;
But let there never be curtain drawn
Between you and me.

Vague dream-head lifted out of the
   ground,
And thing next most diffuse to cloud,
Not all your light tongues talking aloud
Could be profound.

But, tree, I have seen you taken and
   tossed,
And if you had seen me when I slept,
You have seen me when I was taken and
   swept
And all but lost.

[1] Window frame

That day she put our heads together,
Fate had her imagination about her,
Your head so much concerned with outer,
Mine with inner, weather.

—ROBERT FROST

Sweet Are the Uses of Adversity

Sweet are the uses of adversity;
Which, like the toad, ugly and venomous,
Wears yet a precious jewel in his head;
And this our life exempt from public haunt,
Finds tongues in trees, books in the
   running brooks,
Sermons in stones, and good in
   everything.

  —WILLIAM SHAKESPEARE,
    As You Like It, Act 2, Scene 1

For Every Thing There Is a Season

To every thing there is a season, and a time
to every purpose under the heaven:
A time to be born, and a time to die; a time
to plant, and a time to pluck up that
which is planted;
A time to kill, and a time to heal; a time to
break down, and a time to build up;
A time to weep, and a time to laugh; a time
to mourn, and a time to dance;
A time to cast away stones, and a time to
gather stones together; a time to embrace, and a time to refrain from embrac-
ing;
A time to get, and a time to lose; a time to
keep, and a time to cast away;
A time to rend, and a time to sew; a time to
keep silence, and a time to speak;
A time to love, and a time to hate; a time of
war, and a time of peace.
What profit hath he that worketh in that
wherein he laboreth?

I have seen the travail[1], which God hath given the sons of men to be exercised in it.

He hath made every thing beautiful in his time: also he hath set the world in their heart, so that no man can find out the work that God maketh from the beginning to the end.

—Ecclesiastes, 3:1–11 (KJV)

[1] Toil

JUSTICE

THE VIRTUE JUSTICE, at first glance, is easy to understand and appreciate. Almost everyone wants justice for those who are victimized and oppressed. People generally maintain that justice must be fair and equal and must respect individual rights, even though the process of accomplishing justice can be complicated. What is fair to one person in one situation may create inequality for another person in a different situation. Yet justice must be the same for all, whether it concerns laws or moral duties. The famous image of justice as a blindfolded woman holding scales expresses the weighing of facts and impartial aspects of justice.

63

When Aristotle described justice he began by defining *injustice:* unfair laws, the denial of people's rights, and the abuse of authority. When justice is mocked or denied, anger and suffering inevitably follow, sometimes in deeply destructive proportions. Individuals experiencing injustice or communities where human rights are denied become afraid, wrathful, despairing, and cynical.

Plato defined justice directly. He said, "Justice is giving to each what is proper or due to it." To him, justice meant meeting obligations. Every institution and individual has certain obligations owed to others which must be met fairly, equally, and impartially. An employer is required to give workers the pay and benefits agreed upon. The state is expected to give its citizens protection from harm and to bring criminals to justice. Schools must provide education for their students. Obligations go two ways: workers must fulfill their work agreements, citizens must obey the law and pay taxes, students are expected to comply with their teachers' instructions.

Judaism, throughout the centuries, has been a standard-bearer for justice. Its

Scriptures, traditions, and teachings emphasize the sanctity of human life and freedom, and the kinship of the human race. God is called "the Father of all mercies," and "the God of justice." Judaism teaches that all people have a moral duty toward their neighbors. Justice requires the protection and defense of the weak and cries out for equality and order in relationships between classes, peoples, organizations, and countries. Justice calls for feeding and clothing the poor because the right to life itself is due them. This ideal of justice is captured in the Golden Rule, "Do unto others as you would have others do unto you," and in Jesus' words, "Love thy neighbor as thyself."

The New Testament concept of justice agrees with the Greek general sense of "what is right, or as it should be." New Testament justice (often translated "righteousness") includes the proper recognition of humankind's duty toward God and toward other people. The poet-priest John Donne said, "No man is an island." This idea is strongly present in Scripture where justice envisions the human family as bound together in its pain and triumphs. Just persons, laws, and institutions reach out to seek the reconciliation of angry and injured people, to restore what is rightly theirs, to protect the disadvantaged, and to seek healing and amends for the victims of injustice.

Poets write with imagination and power about the unity of humankind, the need for people to care for one another, and of a vision of a just world, in Langston Hughes' words, "Where wretchedness will hang its head, and joy, like a pearl, Attend the needs of all mankind."

I Dream a World

I dream a world where man
No other will scorn,
Where love will bless the earth
And peace its paths adorn.
I dream a world where all
Will know sweet freedom's way,
Where greed no longer saps the soul
Nor avarice blights our day.
A world I dream where black or white,
Whatever race you bed,
Will share the bounties of the earth
And every man is free,
Where wretchedness will hang its head,
And joy, like a pearl,
Attend the needs of all mankind.
Of such I dream—
Our world!

   —LANGSTON HUGHES

From Lincoln's Own Words

I believe the will of God prevails;
Without Him all human reliance is vain;
Without the assistance of that Divine
    Being I cannot succeed;
With that assistance I cannot fail.
I believe I am a humble instrument in the
    hands of our Heavenly Father;
I desire that all my works and acts may be
    according to His will;
and that it may be so, I give thanks to the
    Almighty and seek His aid.
I believe in praise to Almighty God, the
    beneficent Creator and Ruler of the
    Universe.

—ABRAHAM LINCOLN

from *We and They*

Father, Mother, and Me,
Sister and Auntie say
All the people like us are We,
And everyone else is They.
And They live over the sea,
While We live over the way,
But—would you believe it?—
They look upon We
As only a sort of They!

All good people agree,
And all good people say,
All nice people like Us, are We
And everyone else is They:
But if you cross over the sea
Instead of over the way,
You may end by (think of it!)
Looking on We
As only a sort of They!

—RUDYARD KIPLING

69

The Children of the Poor

Hugo was the preeminent French literary figure of the nineteenth century. Today he is well-known for his novel Les Misérables. *In this poem he reflects on the terrible injustice of child poverty.*

Take heed of this small child of earth;
He is great; he hath in him God most
   high.
Children before their fleshly birth
Are lights above in the blue sky.

In our light, bitter world of wrong
They come; God gives us them awhile.
His speech is in their stammering tongue,
And His forgiveness in their smile.

Their sweet light rests upon our eyes.
Alas, their right to joy is plain.
If they are hungry, Paradise
Weeps, and, if cold, Heaven thrills with
   pain.

The want that saps their sinless flower
Speaks judgment on sin's ministers.
Man holds an angel in his power.
Ah, deep in Heaven what thunder stirs,

When God seeks out these tender things
Whom in the shadow where we sleep
He sends us clothed about with wings,
And finds them ragged babes that weep!

—Victor Hugo

System

Every night my prayers I say,
And get my dinner every day;
And every day that I've been good,
I get an orange after food.

The child that is not clean and neat,
With lots of toys and things to eat,
He is a naughty child, I'm sure—
Or else his dear papa is poor.

—ROBERT LOUIS STEVENSON

Make Me Poet Laureate

Make me poet laureate
For the world that writhes in pain
For the child sucked out of the womb
For the prisoner in chains

For those who die in thousands
While the rich sort out their scores
For the unknown disappeared
In those boring foreign wars.

Make me poet laureate
For the stranger in the land
For the daughter who is raped
At her father's evil hand

For the runaway who sleeps
On a mattress made of stone
For the worker out of work
Left to waste away at home.

Make me poet laureate
For the victim no one hears
For every child that's battered
While its screams are gagged by fear

For those too weak to argue
For those who have no tongue
For those too old to matter
In a world which loves the young.

Make me poet laureate
For the beggar at the gate
For those who cry for justice
But are told they have to wait.

Not for presidents and queens
Who are overwhelmed by choice,
But for those whose mouths are
   stopped—
Those who can't afford a voice.

 —STEVE TURNER

Things That Never Die

Best known for the timeless stories and comic characters in his novels, Dickens's writings expressed his deep compassion for the poor in Victorian England. He continues to challenge the consciences of modern readers.

The pure, the bright, the beautiful
that stirred our hearts in youth,
The impulses to wordless prayer,
The streams of love and truth,
The longing after something lost,
The spirit's longing cry,
The striving after better hopes—
These things can never die.

The timid hand stretched forth to aid
A brother in his need;
A kindly word in grief's dark hour
That proves a friend indeed;
The plea for mercy softly breathed,
When justice threatens high,
The sorrow of a contrite heart—
These things shall never die.

Let nothing pass, for every hand
Must find some work to do,
Lose not a chance to waken love—
Be firm and just and true.
So shall a light that cannot fade
Beam on thee from on high,
And angel voices say to thee—
"These things shall never die."

—CHARLES DICKENS

The Beatitudes

Blessed are the poor in spirit: for theirs is the kingdom of heaven.

Blessed are they that mourn: for they shall be comforted.

Blessed are the meek: for they shall inherit the earth.

Blessed are they which do hunger and thirst after righteousness: for they shall be filled.

Blessed are the merciful: for they shall obtain mercy.

Blessed are the pure in heart: for they shall see God.

Blessed are the peacemakers: for they shall be called the children of God.

Blessed are they which are persecuted for righteousness' sake: for theirs is the kingdom of heaven.

—Matthew 5:3–10 (KJV)

(Belshazzar Had a Letter)

The book of Daniel describes a feast held by Belshazzar, co-ruler of the evil Babylonian empire. During the banquet he used sacred vessels stolen from the temple in Jerusalem, thus defiling them. Suddenly the fingers of a human hand appeared before his eyes and wrote a message of his doom on the palace wall.

Belshazzar had a Letter—
He never had but one—
Belshazzar's Correspondent
Concluded and begun
In that immortal Copy
The Conscience of us all
Can read without its Glasses
On Revelation's Wall—

—EMILY DICKINSON

Good King Wenceslas

Wenceslas, who died in 929, was a pious King of Bohemia, recognized in the eleventh century as the patron saint of Bohemia, now the Czech Republic. Vaclav is the Czech form of his name. The poem has become a well-known Christmas carol.

Good King Wenceslas looked out,
On the Feast of Stephen,
When the snow lay round about,
Deep, and crisp and even:
Brightly shone the moon that night,
Though the frost was cruel,
When a poor man came in sight,
Gathering winter fuel.

"Hither, page, and stand by me,
If thou know'st it, telling,
Yonder peasant who is he?
Where and what his dwelling?
"Sire he lives a good league hence,
Underneath the mountain;
Right against the forest fence,
By St. Agnes' fountain."

"Bring me flesh and bring me wine,
Bring me pine logs hither;
Thou and I shall see him dine,
When we bear them thither."
Page and monarch forth they went,
Forth they went together;
Through the rude wind's wild lament,
And the bitter weather.

"Sire, the night is darker now,
And the wind blows stronger;
Fails my heart, I know not how,
I can go no longer."
"Mark my footsteps, good my page!
Tread thou in them boldly;
Thou shalt find the winter's rage
Freeze thy blood less coldly."

In his master's steps he trod,
Where the snow lay dinted;
Heat was in the very sod
Which the saint had printed.
Therefore, Christian folk, be sure,
Wealth or rank possessing,
Ye who now will bless the poor,
Shall yourselves find blessing.

—JOHN MASON NEALE

The Violinist

In Dresden, in the square one day,
His face of parchment, seamed and grey,
With wheezy bow and proffered hat,
An old blind violinist sat.

Like one from whose worn heart the heat
Of life had long ago retired,
He played to the unheeding street
Until the thin old hands were tired.

Few marked the player how he played
Or how the child beside his knee
Besought the passers-by for aid
So softly and so wistfully.

A stranger passed. The little hand
Went forth, so often checked and
     spurned.
The stranger wavered, came to stand,
Looked round with absent eyes and
     turned.

He saw the sightless, withered face,
The tired old hands, the whitened hair,
The child with such a mournful grace,
The little features pinched and spare.

"I have no money, but," said he,
Give me the violin and bow,
I'll play a little, we shall see,
Whether the gold will come or no."

With lifted brow and flashing eyes
He faced the noisy street and played.
The people turned in quick surprise,
And every foot drew near and stayed.

First from the shouting bow he sent
A summons, an impetuous call;
Then some old store of grief long pent
Broke from his heart and mastered all.

The tumult sank at his command,
The passing wheels were hushed and
    stilled:
The burning soul, the sweeping hand
A sacred ecstasy fulfilled.

The darkness of the outer strife
The weariness, the child within,
The giant wrongfulness of life,
Leaped storming from the violin.

The jingling round of pleasure broke,
Gay carriages were drawn near,
And all the proud and haughty folk
Leaned from their cushioned seats to
    hear.

And then the player changed his tone
And wrought another miracle
Of music, half a prayer, half moan,
A cry exceeding sorrowful.

A strain of pity for the weak,
The poor that fall without a cry,
The common hearts that never speak,
But break beneath the press and die.

Throughout the great and silent crowd
The music fell on human ears,
And many kindly heads were bowed,
And many eyes were warm with tears.

"And now your gold," the player cried,
"While love is master of your mood;"
He bowed, and turned, and slipped aside,
And vanished in the multitude.

And all the people flocked at that,
The money like a torrent rolled,
Until the grey old battered hat
Was bursting to the brim with gold.

And loudly as the giving grew,
The question rose on every part,
If any named or any knew
The stranger with so great a heart.

Or what the moving wonder meant,
Such playing never heard before;
A lady from her carriage leant,
And murmured softly, "It was Spohr[1]."

—ARCHIBALD LAMPMAN

[1] Ludwig Spohr, 1784–1859, great German composer, conductor, and violinist

Magnus Est Veritas[1]

This poem was a favorite of Robert Frost.

Here in this little Bay,
Full of tumultuous life and great repose,
Where, twice a day,
The purposeless, glad ocean comes and
   goes,
Under high cliffs, and far from the huge
   town,
I sit me down.
For want of me the world's course will not
   fail;
When all its work is done. The lie shall rot;
The truth is great, and shall prevail,
When none cares whether it prevail or not.

—COVENTRY PATMORE

[1] Great is Truth

Refugee in America

There are words like *Freedom*
Sweet and wonderful to say.
On my heart-strings freedom sings
All day every day.

There are words like *Liberty*
That almost make me cry.
If you had known what I knew
You would know why.

—LANGSTON HUGHES

Message to Siberia

Deep in the Siberian mine,
Keep your patience proud;
The bitter toil shall not be lost,
The rebel thought unbowed.

The sister of misfortune, Hope,
In the under-darkness dumb
Speaks joyful courage to your heart:
The day desired will come.

And love and friendship pour to you
Across the darkened doors,
Even as round your galley-beds
My free music pours.

The heaving-hanging chains will fall,
The walls will crumble at a word;
And Freedom greet you in the light,
And brothers give you back the sword.

—ALEKSANDR PUSHKIN, translated by Max
Eastman

The New Colossus

Engraved on a plaque in the Statue of Liberty

Not like the brazen giant of Greek fame,
With conquering limbs astride from land to
    land;
Here at our sea-washed, sunset gates
    shall stand
A mighty woman with a torch, whose
    flame
Is the imprisoned lightning, and her name
Mother of Exiles. From her beacon-hand
Glows world-wide welcome; her mild eyes
    command
The air-bridged harbor that twin cities
    frame.
"Keep, ancient lands, your storied pomp!"
    cries she
With silent lips. "Give me your tired, your
    poor,
Your huddled masses yearning to breathe
    free,
The wretched refuse of your teeming
    shore,

Send these, the homeless, tempest-tost,
  to me,
I lift my lamp beside the golden door!"

—Emma Lazarus

Truth Never Dies

Truth never dies. The ages come and go.
The mountains wear away, the stars retire.
Destruction lays earth's mighty cities low;
And empires, states and dynasties expire;
But caught and handed onward by the
   wise,
     Truth never dies.

Though unreceived and scoffed at through
   the years;
Though made the butt of ridicule and jest;
Though held aloft for mockery and jeers,
Denied by those of transient power
   possessed,
Insulted by the insolence of lies,
     Truth never dies.

It answers not. It does not take offence,
But with a mighty silence bides its time;
As some great cliff that braves the
   elements
And lifts through all the storms its head
   sublime,
It ever stands, uplifted by the wise;
     And never dies.

As rests the Sphinx amid Egyptian sands;
As looms on high the snowy peak and
  crest;
As firm and patient as Gibraltar stands,
So truth, unwearied, waits the era blest
When men shall turn to it with great
  surprise.
   Truth never dies.

   —ANONYMOUS

Abraham Lincoln Walks at Midnight

*Between 1906 and 1912, Lindsay toured the
United States on foot, giving readings of his
poetry in return for food and lodging, seeking
to revive the art of oral poetry.*

It is portentous, and a thing of state
That here at midnight, in our little town
A mourning figure walks, and will not rest,
Near the old court-house pacing up and
down,

Or by his homestead, or in the shadowed
yards
He lingers where his children used to play,
Or through the market, on the well-worn
stones
He stalks until the dawn-stars burn away.

A bronzed, lank man! His suit of ancient
black,
A famous high top-hat and plain worn
shawl
Make him the quaint great figure that men
love,
The prairie-lawyer, master of us all.

He cannot sleep upon his hillside now.
He is among us:—as in times before!
And we who toss and lie awake for long
Breathe deep, and start, to see him pass
the door.

His head is bowed. He thinks on men and
kings.
Yea, when the sick world cries, how can
he sleep?
Too many peasants fight, they know not
why,
Too many homesteads in black terror
weep.

The sins of all the war-lords burn his
heart.
He sees the dreadnaughts[1] scouring every
main[2].
He carries on his shawl-wrapped
shoulders now
The bitterness, the folly and the pain.

[1] A heavily armed battleship
[2] Open ocean

He cannot rest until a spirit-dawn
Shall come;—the shining hope of Europe
   free:
The league of sober folk, the Workers'
   Earth,
Bringing long peace to Cornland, Alp and
   Sea.

It breaks his heart that kings must murder
   still,
That all his hours of travail here for men
Seem yet in vain. And who will bring white
   peace
That he may sleep upon his hill again?

   —VACHEL LINDSAY

Justice in the Bible

When justice is done, it is a joy to the righteous, but dismay to evildoers.

—Proverbs 21:15

Learn to do good; seek justice, rescue the oppressed, defend the orphan, plead for the widow.

—Isaiah 1:17

But let justice roll down like waters, and righteousness like an ever-flowing stream.

—Amos 5:24

He has told you, O mortal, what is good; and what does the Lord require of you but to do justice, and to love kindness, and to walk humbly with your God?

—Micah 6:8

The weightier matters of the law [are] justice
and mercy and faith.

—Matthew 23:23

Not Waving but Drowning

We have a moral duty to help others, but all too often people's cries for help are disregarded or misunderstood. The poem suggests that the man's friends were cheerfully oblivious to his life-long distress.

Nobody heard him, the dead man,
But still he lay moaning:
I was much further out than you thought
And not waving but drowning.

Poor chap, he always loved larking
And now he's dead
It must have been too cold for him his
    heart gave way,
They said.

Oh, no, no, no, it was too cold always
(Still the dead one lay moaning)
I was much too far out all my life
And not waving but drowning.

—STEVIE SMITH

Frederick Douglass

Born a slave in 1817, Douglass became the most famous of all black Abolitionists as well as a great American orator.

When it is finally ours, this freedom, this
    liberty,
this beautiful and terrible thing, needful to
    man as air,
usable as earth; when it belongs at last to
    our children,
when it is truly instinct, brain matter,
    diastole, systole,[1]
reflex action; when it is finally won; when
    it is more
than the gaudy mumbo jumbo of
    politicians:
this man, this Douglass, this former slave,
    this Negro

---

[1] The in-and-out pumping of the heart

beaten to his knees, exiled, visioning a
    world
where none is lonely, none hunted, alien,
this man, superb in love and logic, this
    man
shall be remembered. Oh, not with
    statues' rhetoric,
not with legends and poems and wreaths
    of bronze alone,
but with the lives grown out of his life, the
    lives
fleshing his dream of the beautiful, needful
    thing.

—ROBERT HAYDEN

Fires

As the poet drowses by his fire, his imagination creates glowing pictures in the flames. However, when he shuts his eyes, his pleasant revery is startled by an image of a miner, working in unjust, subhuman conditions as he digs his coal.

Snug in my easy chair,
I stirred the fire to flame.
Fantastically fair,
The flickering fancies came,
Born of the heart's desire:
Amber woodland streaming;
Topaz islands dreaming;
Sunset-cities gleaming,
Spire on burning spire;
Ruddy-windowed taverns;
Sunshine-spilling wines;
Crystal-lighted caverns
Of Golcanda's[1] mines;
Summers, unreturning;
Passion's crater yearning;
Troy, the ever-burning;

---

[1] An ancient city in India, now deserted, once famous for its wealth

Shelley's lustral pyre;
Dragon-eyes, unsleeping;
Witches' cauldrons leaping;
Golden galleys[2] sweeping
Out from sea-walled Tyre:
Fancies fugitive and fair,
Flashed with singing through the air;
Till, dazzled by the drowsy glare,
I shut my eyes to heat and light:
And saw, in sudden night,
Crouched in the dripping dark,
With streaming shoulders stark,
The man who hews the coal to feed my
   fire.

—WILFRID GIBSON

[2] A large ship of the Middle Ages, propelled by sails and oars

Judgment Day

This poem is a prayer of repentance for deliberately shutting out the world's suffering.

Yes, that's how I was,
I know that face,
That bony figure
Without grace
Of flesh or limb;
In health happy,
Careless of the claim
Of the world's sick
Or the world's poor;
In pain craven—
Lord, breathe once more
On that sad mirror,
Let me be lost
In mist for ever
Rather than own
Such bleak reflections.
Let me go back
On my two knees
Slowly to undo
The knot of life
That was tied there.

—R. S. THOMAS

To Keep a True Lent

For many Christians, Lent is a forty-day penitential period of prayer and fasting that precedes Easter. The poet observes that a true Lent produces acts of mercy and reconciliation, true qualities of justice.

Is this a Fast, to keep
The larder lean,
And clean
From fat of veals and sheep?

Is it to quit the dish
Of flesh, yet still
To fill
The platter high with fish?

Is it to fast an hour,
Or ragg'd to go,
Or show
A downcast look and sour?

No: 'tis a Fast to dole
Thy sheaf of wheat
And meat,
Unto the hungry soul.

It is to fast from strife,
From old debate
And hate;
To circumcise thy life.

To show a heart grief-rent;
To starve thy sin,
Not bin[1]:
And that's to keep thy Lent.

    —ROBERT HERRICK

[1] A place for food storage

from *Letter to the Governors,*
June 8, 1783

I now make it my earnest prayer
that God would have you,
and the state over which you preside, in
   His holy protection;
that He would incline the hearts of the
   citizens
to cultivate a spirit of subordination and
   obedience to the government;
to entertain a brotherly affection and love
   for one another,
for their fellow citizens of the United
   States at large
and particularly for their brethren who
   have served in the field;
and finally that He would graciously be
   pleased to dispose us all to do justice,
to love mercy, and to demean ourselves
   with charity and humility,
and a pacific[1] temper of mind, which were
   characteristics of the Divine Author of
   our blessed religion,

[1] Peaceful

and without an humble imitation of whose
   example in these things,
we can never hope to be a happy nation.

—GEORGE WASHINGTON

from *The Vision of Sir Launfal*

In the biblical parable of the Sheep and the Goats (Matthew 25:32–32:46), Jesus teaches that whatever good works are done for the needy, they are done for Him.

And the voice that was softer than silence
    said,
"Lo, it is I, be not afraid!
In many climes, without avail,
Thou has spent thy life for the Holy Grail[1];
Behold, it is here—this cup which thou
Didst fill at the streamlet for me but now;
This crust is my body broken for thee,
This water his blood that died on the tree;
The Holy Supper is kept, in deed,
In whatso we share with another's need;
Not what we give, but what we share,
For the gift without the giver is bare;
Who gives himself with his alms feeds
    three,
Himself, his hungering neighbor, and me."

—JAMES RUSSELL LOWELL

[1] A legend associated with the cup used at the Last Supper. The blood from Christ's wounds were said to have been collected in the cup, which then had miraculous powers.

For Whom the Bell Tolls

It was the custom in Europe, before a funeral, for the bells of a church to toll to signal to everyone that someone had died.

No man is an island, entire of itself;
every man is a piece of the continent, a
    part of the main.
If a clod be washed away by the sea,
Europe is the less, as well as if a
    promontory were,
as well as if a manor of thy friend's or of
    thine own were:
any man's death diminishes me, because I
    am involved in mankind,
and therefore never send to know for
    whom the bell tolls;
it tolls for thee.

    —JOHN DONNE

The Guest

Washed into the doorway
by the wake of the traffic,
he wears humanity
like a third-hand shirt
—blackened with enough
of Manhattan's dirt to sprout
a tree, or poison one.
His empty hand has led him
where he has come to.
Our differences claim us.
He holds out his hand,
in need of all that's mine.

And so we're joined, as deep
as son and father. His life
is offered me to choose.

Shall I begin servitude
to him? Let this cup pass.
Who am I? But charity must
suppose, knowing no better,
that this is a man fallen
among thieves, or come
to this strait by no fault

—that our difference
is not a judgment,
though I can afford to eat
and am made his judge.

I am, I nearly believe,
the Samaritan[1] who fell
into the ambush of his heart
on the way to another place.
My stranger waits, his hand
held out like something to read,
as though its emptiness
is an accomplishment.
I give him a smoke and the price
of a meal, no more
—not sufficient kindness
or believable sham.
I paid him to remain strange
to my threshold and table,
to permit me to forget him—
knowing I won't. He's the guest
of my knowing, though not asked.

—WENDELL BERRY

[1] Jesus' parable of the good Samaritan who had compassion on
the man who fell among thieves, recounted in the Gospel of Luke,
10:30–35.

Briefly It Enters, and Briefly Speaks

In the New Testament, Jesus used metaphors such as "I am the door," "I am the good shepherd," "I am the bread," "I am the light." The poet beautifully extends the Biblical metaphors to include images that show Christ's sense of justice and compassion for the hungry and prisoners.

I am the blossom pressed in a book,
found again after two hundred years . . .

I am the maker, the lover, the keeper . . .

When the young girl who starves
sits down to a table
she will sit beside me . . .

I am food on the prisoner's plate . . .

I am water rushing to the well-head,
filling the pitcher until it spills . . .

I am the patient gardener
of the dry and weedy garden . . .

I am the stone step,
the latch, and the working hinge . . .

I am the heart contracted with joy . . .
The longest hair, white
before the rest . . .

I am the basket of fruit
presented to the widow . . .

I am the musk rose opening
unattended, the fern on the boggy
  summit . . .

I am the one whose love
overcomes you, already with you
when you think to call my name . . .

    —Jane Kenyon

Stanzas on Freedom

Is true Freedom but to break
Fetters for our own dear sake,
And, with leathern hearts, forget
That we owe mankind a debt?
No! True freedom is to share
All the chains our brothers wear,
And, with heart and hand, to be
Earnest to make others free!

They are slaves who fear to speak
For the fallen and the weak;
They are slaves who will not choose
Hatred, scoffing, and abuse,
Rather than in silence shrink
From the truth they needs must think:
They are slaves who dare not be
In the right with two or three.

—JAMES RUSSELL LOWELL

The Quality of Mercy

The quality of mercy is not strain'd,
It droppeth as the gentle rain from heaven
Upon the place beneath: It is twice blest;
It blesses him that gives, and him that
    takes:
'Tis mightiest in the mightiest: it becomes
The throned monarch better than his
    crown;
His sceptre shows the force of temporal
    power,
The attribute to awe and majesty,
Wherein doth sit the dread and fear of
    kings;
But mercy is above this sceptred sway;
It is enthroned in the hearts of kings,
It is an attribute to God himself;
And earthly power doth then show likest
    God's
When mercy seasons justice.

—WILLIAM SHAKESPEARE,
    Merchant of Venice, Act 4, Scene 1

The Inner Light

Milton reflects on the fact that a clear con-
science gives light and pleasure, but a guilty
conscience imprisons a person in darkness.

He that has light within his own clear
   breast
May sit i' the center, and enjoy bright day:
But he that hides a dark soul and foul
   thoughts
Benighted[1] walks under the midday sun;
Himself his own dungeon.

     —JOHN MILTON

[1] Overtaken by darkness

The Ultimate Justice of the People

What constitutes the bulwark of our own
   liberty and independence?
It is not our frowning battlements, our
   bristling seacoast, our army and navy.
Our reliance is in the love of liberty which
   God has planted in us.
Our defense is in the spirit which prizes
   liberty as the heritage of all men in all
   lands everywhere.
Destroy this spirit, and we all have planted
   the seeds of despotism at our own
   doors.
Those who deny freedom to others
   deserve it not for themselves,
And under a just God, cannot long retain
   it.
This country, with its institutions, belongs
   to the people who inhabit it.
Why should there not be a patient
   confidence in the ultimate justice of the
   people?
Is there any better or equal hope in the
   world?

—ABRAHAM LINCOLN

Great Is Justice!
from Great Are the Myths

Great is Justice!
Justice is not settled by legislators and
laws—it is in the Soul,
It cannot be varied by statutes, any more
than love, pride, the attraction of
gravity, can,
It is immutable—it does not depend on
majorities—majorities or what not come
at last before the same passionless and
exact tribunal.

For justice are the grand natural lawyers
and perfect judges—it is in their Souls,
It is well assorted—they have not studied
for nothing—the great includes the less,
They rule on the highest grounds—they
oversee all eras, states, administrations.

The perfect judge fears nothing—he could
go front to front before God,
Before the perfect judge all shall stand
back—life and death shall stand back—
heaven and hell shall stand back.

—WALT WHITMAN

COURAGE

DURING THE NAZI OCCUPATION of his country, the King of Denmark gave the order that a Nazi flag flying over a Danish public building be taken down. The German commandant refused. "Then a Danish soldier will take it down," said the King. "He will be shot," returned the commandant. "I think not," replied the King, "for I shall be the soldier." The flag was taken down.

Courage finds its center, not in an individual's reason, but in a person's inner spirit and resolve. The courageous person confronts danger, even to the point of giving up life itself, in order to defend what is good and true.

In the order of the virtues, courage is the

third of the four "natural" or moral virtues. It is placed third because of the Greek idea that courage flows from wisdom and justice. The Greeks taught that the courageous individual must first have the wisdom to consider an action and its risk, to count the cost. An *impulsive* act in a dangerous situation is not evidence of the moral virtue of courage.

The Greek philosophers taught that justice is the second component of courage. Just because a person evaluates a risky course of action and then undertakes it does not mean that the person is courageous. The risk to be taken must be for a moral cause. Reckless and violent gang members who endanger their lives to attack a street enemy do not possess the virtue of courage. Their action may be dangerous, but it is not courageous because it does not encompass wise thought or moral good.

In the Christian era, the understanding of courage extended to include bravery in facing dangers to the soul as well as the body. The biblical teaching that Christians struggle with spiritual forces of evil admonishes believers to make a stand for truth, righteousness, and peace. Christianity also recognizes that life in this world includes suffering and injury. The courageous individual, as seen in Scripture, is one who withstands temptation and accepts life's difficulties with patience.

Some of the poems in this section are written by true heroes who express their deepest fears and aspirations. Others are by poets who celebrate human courage and resolve in everyday experiences. The last stanza of Amelia Earhart's poem "Courage" observes, "Each time we make a choice, we pay with courage . . ."

Courage

Courage is the price that Life exacts for
  granting peace,
The soul that knows it not
Knows no release from little things:

Knows not the livid loneliness of fear,
Nor mountain heights where bitter joy can
  hear
The sound of wings.

How can Life grant us boon of living,
  compensate
For dull gray ugliness and pregnant hate
Unless we dare

The soul's dominion? Each time we make
  a choice, we pay
With courage to behold resistless day
And count it fair.

—AMELIA EARHART

I Am Not Bound to Win

I am not bound to win,
But I am bound to be true.
I am not bound to succeed,
But I am bound to live up to what light I
  have.
I must stand with anybody that stands
  right;
Stand with him while he is right,
And part with him when he goes wrong.

—ABRAHAM LINCOLN

Mother to Son

Well, son, I'll tell you:
Life for me ain't been no crystal stair.
It's had tacks in it,
And splinters,
And boards torn up,
And places with no carpet on the floor—
Bare.
But all the time
I'se been a-climbing on,
And reachin' landin's,
And turnin' corners,
And sometimes goin' in the dark
Where there ain't been no light.
So boy, don't you turn back.
Don't you set down on the steps
'Cause you find it's kinder hard.
Don't you fall now—
For I'se still goin' honey,
I'se still climbin',
And life for me ain't been no crystal stair.

—LANGSTON HUGHES

A Psalm Requesting Faith

Give me courage Lord
to take risks
not the usual ones
respected
necessary
relatively safe
but those I could avoid
the go for broke ones.
I need courage
not just because
I may fall on my face
or worse
but others seeing me
a sorry spectacle
if it should happen
will say
he didn't know what he was doing
or he's foolhardy
or he's old enough to know
you lead from the side
instead of letting yourself be caught
in a wild stampede.
Give me courage Lord
to take unnecessary risks
live at tension

instead of opting out.
Give me the guts to put up
instead of shutting up.

—Joseph Bayly

Believe Me

Believe me, it was often thus:
In solitary cells, on winter nights
A sudden sense of joy and warmth
And a resounding note of love,
And then, unsleeping, I would know
A-huddle by an icy wall:
Someone is thinking of me now,
Petitioning the Lord for me.
My dear ones, thank you all
Who did not falter, who believed in us!
In the most fearful prison hour
We probably would not have passed
Through everything—from end to end,
Our heads held high, unbowed—
Without your valiant hearts
To light our path.

—IRINA RATUSHINSKAYA

I Bind unto Myself

I bind unto myself today
The power of God to hold and lead,
His eye to watch, his might to stay,
His ear to hearken to my need.
The wisdom of my God to teach,
His hand to guide,
His shield to ward;
The word of God to give me speech,
His heavenly host to be my guard.

—ST. PATRICK

To Die

To die . . . so young to die . . . no, no,
    not I.
I love the warm of sunny skies,
Light, songs, shining eyes.
I want no war, no battle cry—
No, no . . . Not I.

But if it must be that I live today
With blood and death on every hand,
Praised be He for the grace, I'll say
To live, if I should die this day . . .
Upon your soil, my home, my land.

—HANNAH SENESH, translated by Dorothy
    H. Rochmis

Prayer for Courage

Let me not pray to be sheltered from
    dangers, but to be fearless in facing
    them.
Let me not beg for the stilling of my pain
    but for the heart to conquer it.
Let me not look for allies in life's
    battlefield, but to my own strength.
Let me not crave in anxious fear to be
    saved, but hope for the patience to win
    my freedom.
Grant that I may not be a coward, feeling
    your mercy in my success alone; but let
    me
find the grasp of your hand in my failure.

—RABINDRANATH TAGORE

The Old Stoic[1]

Riches I hold in light esteem,
And Love I laugh to scorn;
And lust of fame was but a dream
That vanished with the morn:

And if I pray, the only prayer
That moves my lips for me
Is "Leave the heart that now I bear,
And give me liberty!"

Yes, as my swift days near their goal,
'Tis all that I implore;
Through life and death a chainless soul,
With courage to endure.

—EMILY BRONTË

---

[1] Stoicism was a philosophical movement beginning in the third century B.C. which lasted about five hundred years. It adapted the ideals of virtue, endurance, and self-sufficiency taught by Socrates.

from *Yes*

It often takes courage to answer "Yes" to life,
but an affirming, optimistic attitude can result
in delightful outcomes.

Some go local
Some go express
Some can't wait
To answer Yes.

Some complain
Of strain and stress
Their answer may be
No for Yes.

Some like failure
Some like success
Some like Yes Yes
Yes Yes Yes.

Open your eyes,
Dream but don't guess.
Your biggest surprise
Comes after Yes.

—MURIEL RUKEYSER

Sandinista Avioncitos

The little airplanes of the heart
with their brave little propellers
What can they do
against the winds of darkness
even as butterflies are beaten back
by hurricanes
yet do not die
They lie in wait wherever
they can hide and hang
their fine wings folded
and when the killer-wind dies
they flutter forth again
into the new-blown light
live as leaves

—LAWRENCE FERLINGHETTI

Courage in the Bible

Be strong and bold; have no fear or dread of them, because it is the Lord your God who goes with you; he will not fail you or forsake you.

—Deuteronomy 31:6

I hereby command you: Be strong and courageous; do not be frightened or dismayed, for the Lord your God is with you wherever you go.

—Joshua 1:9

Wait for the Lord; be strong, and let your heart take courage; wait for the Lord!

—Psalm 27:14

The Song My Paddle Sings

This poem by a famous Mohawk First Nation poet is beloved in Canada. The canoe's progress down the river is a metaphor of life's changing and sometimes precarious journey.

West wind, blow from your prairie nest
Blow from the mountains, blow from the
    west.
The sail is idle, the sailor too;
O! wind of the west, we wait for you.
Blow, blow!
I have wooed you so,
But never a favor you bestow.
You rock your cradle the hills between,
But scorn to notice my white lateen.[1]

I stow the sail, unship the mast:
I wooed you long but my wooing's past;
My paddle will lull you into rest.
O! drowsy wind of the drowsy west,
Sleep, sleep,
By your mountain steep,

---

[1] A triangular sail

Or down where the prairie grasses
   sweep!
Now fold in slumber your laggard wings,
For soft is the song my paddle sings.

August is laughing across the sky,
Laughing while paddle, canoe and I,
Drift, drift,
Where the hills uplift
On either side of the current swift.
The river rolls in its rocky bed;
My paddle is plying its way ahead;
Dip, dip,
While the waters flip
In foam as over their breast we slip.

And oh, the river runs swifter now;
The eddies circle about my bow.
Swirl, swirl!
How the ripples curl
In many a dangerous pool awhirl!

And forward far the rapids roar,
Fretting their margin for evermore.
Dash, dash,
With a mighty crash,
They seethe, and boil, and bound, and
   splash.

Be strong, O paddle! be brave, canoe!
The reckless waves you must plunge
   into.
Reel, reel.
On your trembling keel,
But never a fear my craft will feel.

We've raced the rapid, we're far ahead!
The river slips through its silent bed.
Sway, sway,
As the bubbles spray
And fall in tinkling tunes away.

And up on the hills against the sky,
A fir tree rocking its lullaby,
Swings, swings,
Its emerald wings,
Swelling the song that my paddle sings.

—PAULINE JOHNSON

Cowards

These well-known lines are spoken by Julius Caesar after he is warned of omens of disaster.

Cowards die many times before their
   deaths:
The valiant never taste of death but once.
Of all the wonders that I yet have heard,
It seems to me most strange that men
   should fear,
Seeing that death, a necessary end,
Will come, when it will come.

  —WILLIAM SHAKESPEARE,
    Julius Caesar, Act 2, Scene 2

Life

Life, believe, is not a dream,
So dark as sages say;
Oft a little morning rain
Foretells a pleasant day:
Sometimes there are clouds of gloom,
But these are transient all;
If the shower will make the roses bloom,
Oh, why lament its fall?
Rapidly, merrily,
Life's sunny hours flit by,
Gratefully, cheerily,
Enjoy them as they fly.

What though Death at times steps in,
And calls our Best away?
What though Sorrow seems to win,
O'er Hope a heavy sway?
Yet Hope again elastic springs,
Unconquered, though she fell;
Still buoyant are her golden wings,
Still strong to bear us well.
Manfully, fearlessly,

The day of trial bear,
For gloriously, virtuously,
Can courage quell despair!

—CHARLOTTE BRONTË

I Think Continually of Those Who Were Truly Great

I think continually of those who were truly
  great.
Who, from the womb, remembered the
  soul's history
Through corridors of light where the hours
  are suns,
Endless and singing. Whose lovely
  ambition
Was that their lips, still touched with fire,
Should tell of the Spirit, clothed from head
  to foot in song.
And who hoarded from the Spring
  branches
The desires falling across their bodies like
  blossoms.

What is precious is never to forget
The essential delight of the blood drawn
  from ageless springs
Breaking through rocks in worlds before
  our earth.
Never to deny its pleasure in the morning
  simple light

Nor its grave evening demand for love.
Never to allow gradually the traffic to
  smother,
With noise and fog, the flowering of the
  spirit.

Near the snow, near the sun, in the
  highest fields,
See how these names are feted by the
  waving grass
And by the streamers of white cloud
And whispers of wind in the listening sky.
The names of those who in their lives
  fought for life,
Who wore at their hearts the fire's centre.
Born of the sun, they traveled a short
  while towards the sun,
And left the vivid air signed with their
  honour.

—STEPHEN SPENDER

Psalm of Life

Tell me not, in mournful numbers,
Life is but an empty dream!
For the soul is dead that slumbers,
And things are not what they seem.

Life is real! Life is earnest!
And the grave is not its goal;
Dust thou art, to dust returnest,
Was not spoken of the soul.

Not enjoyment and not sorrow
Is our destined end or way;
But to act, that each tomorrow
Finds us further than today.

Art is long, and time is fleeting,
And our hearts, though stout and brave,
Still, like muffled drums, are beating
Funeral marches to the grave.

In the world's broad field of battle,
In the bivouac[1] of life,
Be not like dumb, driven cattle!
Be a hero in the strife!

Trust no future, howe'er pleasant!
Let the dead past bury its dead!
Act—act in the living present!
Heart within, and God overhead!

Lives of great men all remind us
We can make our lives sublime,
And, departing, leave behind us
Footprints on the sand of time—

Footprints, that perhaps another,
Sailing o'er life's solemn main,
A forlorn and shipwrecked brother,
Seeing, shall take heart again.

Let us, then, be up and doing,
With a heart for any fate;
Still achieving, still pursuing,
Learn to labor and to wait.

—HENRY WADSWORTH LONGFELLOW

[1] A temporary encampment made by soldiers in the field

from *Ulysses*

*Ulysses is an epic hero in Greek mythology.
Tennyson's poem celebrates Ulysses's courage and love of adventure that flourished even
in old age.*

I am a part of all that I have met;
Yet all experience is an arch
   wherethrough
Gleams that untraveled world whose
   margin fades
For ever and for ever when I move.
How dull it is to pause, to make an end,
To rust unburnished, not to shine in use!
As though to breathe were life! Life piled
   on life
Were all too little, and of one to me
Little remains; but every hour is saved
From that eternal silence, something
   more,
A bringer of new things;

Come, my friends,
'Tis not too late to seek a newer world.
Push off, and sitting well in order smite

The sounding furrows; for my purpose
    hold
To sail beyond the sunset, and the baths
Of all the western stars, until I die.
It may be that the gulfs will wash us
    down:
It may be we shall touch the Happy
    Isles,
And see the great Achilles[1], whom we
    knew.
Though much is taken, much abides;
    and though
We are not now that strength which in
    the old days
Moved earth and heaven, that which we
    are, we are;
One equal temper of heroic hearts,
Made weak by time and fate, but strong
    in will
To strive, to seek, to find, and not to
    yield.

—ALFRED LORD TENNYSON

[1] In Greek mythology, Achilles was foremost of the heroes who fought in the Trojan War.

from *What Are Years*

The poet asks the question: where does the courage come from that in the face of questions, doubts, misfortune, death, still encourages others and urges the soul to be strong?

What is our innocence,
what is our guilt? All are
naked, none is safe. And whence
is courage: the unanswered question,
the resolute doubt—
dumbly calling, deafly listening—that
in misfortune, even death,
encourages others
and in its defeat, stirs

the soul to be strong?

—MARIANNE MOORE

Approach to a City

Williams, a medical doctor as well as a poet, knew what it was to be "trampled and lined with use." He reflects on the courage it takes in everyday life to be humble, and to serve even when unappreciated.

Getting through with the world—
I never tire of the mystery
of these streets: the three baskets
of dried flowers in the high

bar-room window, the gulls wheeling
above the factory, the dirty
snow—the humility of the snow that
silvers everything and is

trampled and lined with use—yet
falls again, the silent birds
on the still wires of the sky, the blur
of wings as they take off

together. The flags in the heavy
air move against a leaden
ground—the snow
pencilled with the stubble of old

weeds. I never tired of these sights
but refresh myself there
always, for there is small holiness
to be found in braver things.

—WILLIAM CARLOS WILLIAMS

Vitai Lampada[1]

The lessons of courage and determination learned in school on the playing field can light the way through the difficulties of adult life.

There's a breathless hush in the Close to-
night—
Ten to make the match[2] to win—
A bumping pitch and a blinding light,
An hour to play and the last man in.
And it's not for the sake of a ribboned
coat,
Or the selfish hope of a season's fame,
But his Captain's hand on his shoulder
smote—
"Play up! play up! And play the game!"

[1] Lamp of life
[2] Cricket match. An English bat and ball team game

The sand of the desert is sodden red,—
Red with the wreck of a square[3] that
    broke;—
The Gatling's jammed and the Colonel
    dead,
And the regiment blind with dust and
    smoke.
The river of death has brimmed his banks,
And England's far and Honour a name,
But the voice of a schoolboy rallies the
    ranks:
"Play up! play up! and play the game!"

This is the word that year by year,
While in her place the School is set,
Every one of her sons must hear,
And none that hears it dare forget.
This they all with joyful mind
Bear through life like a torch in flame,
And falling fling to the host behind—
"Play up! play up! and play the game!"

—SIR HENRY NEWBOLT

[3] A body of troops drawn up in a square or four-sided formation

from *Passage to India*

Whitman dares his adventuring soul to steer bravely for "the deep waters only," knowing that he will be safe as he asks, "are not all the seas of God?"

Bathe me O God in thee, mounting to
   thee,
I and my soul to range in range of thee.

O Thou transcendent,
Nameless, the fibre and the breath,
Light of the light, shedding forth universes,
   thou center of them,
Thou mightier center of the true, the good,
   the loving,
Thou moral, spiritual fountain—affection's
   source—thou reservoir,
(O pensive soul of me—O thirst
   unsatisfied—waitest not there?
Waitest not haply for us somewhere there
   the Comrade perfect?)
Thou pulse—thou motive of the stars,
   suns, systems,
That, circling, move in order, safe,
   harmonious,

Athwart the shapeless vastness of space,
How should I think, how breathe a single
   breath, how speak, if, out of myself?
I could not launch, to those, superior
   universes?

Sail forth—steer for the deep waters only,
Reckless O soul, exploring, I with thee
   and thou with me,
For we are bound where mariner has not
   yet dared to go,
And we will risk the ship, ourselves and
   all.

O my brave soul!
O farther, farther sail!
O daring joy, but safe! are they not all the
   seas of God?
O farther, farther, farther sail!

   —WALT WHITMAN

Valor

A brave person and a coward can appear similar when things are going well, but when difficulties arise, the coward flees or gives up. The person of true courage prevails when put to the test in the storms of life.

In the reproof of chance
Lies the true proof of men. The sea being
   smooth,
How many shallow bauble[1] boats dare sail
Upon her patient breast, making their way
With those of nobler bulk!
But let the ruffian Boreas[2] once enrage
The gentle Thetis[3], and anon, behold
The strong-ribb'd bark[4] through liquid
   mountains cut,
Bounding between the two most elements
Like Perseus'[5] horse. Where's then the
   saucy boat,

---

[1] A cheap trinket
[2] The North wind
[3] A beloved sea-goddess
[4] Boat
[5] In Greek mythology, Perseus was a hero of many exciting adventures.

Whose weak untimber'd sides but even
now
Co-rivall'd greatness? Either to harbor
fled,
Or made a toast for Neptune.[6] Even so
Doth valor's show and valor's worth, di-
vide
In storms of fortune.

    —WILLIAM SHAKESPEARE,
       Troilus and Cressida, Act 1, Scene 3

[6] Chief god of the sea

December Stillness

December stillness, teach me through
  your trees
That loom along the west, one with the
  land,
The veiled evangel of your mysteries.
While nightfall, sad and spacious, on the
  down[1]
Deepens, and dust imbues me, where I
  stand,
With grave diminishings of green and
  brown,
Speak, roofless nature, your instinctive
  words;
And let me learn your secret from the sky,
Following a flock of steadfast, journeying
  birds
In lone remote migration beating by.
December stillness, crossed by twilight
  roads,
Teach me to travel far and bear my loads.

—SIEGFRIED SASSOON

---

[1] An expanse of rolling, grassy upland used for grazing

MODERATION

THE FIRST THREE moral virtues better the world. Families, communities, and nations are blessed and ennobled by those who are wise, just, and courageous. The virtue moderation, *temperance,* in its majestic power betters, enriches, and fulfills the life of the individual who possesses it. The Greeks exalted moderation as one of the supreme "hinges" of life itself.

The meaning of the word *temperance,* in its journey through the centuries, has come to mean "abstinence from drinking alcoholic beverages." The Greeks would certainly react with surprise and even disdain at such an interpretation of the word. They understood *temperance* to be the great virtue by which a person inwardly centers and orders his or her *entire* life.

It is difficult to find an English word that captures the magnificence of the Greek concept. For the sake of selecting only one word to replace *temperance,* I have chosen *moderation.* Moderation is understood as the use of reason to direct and control human experience. The virtue enjoins the disciplined and reasoned governing of the body's primitive needs, appetites and impulses. The supreme value of this aspect of the virtue can easily be recognized. One has only to see the unfortunate person who is controlled by his or her appetites to see that inner disorder and self-destruction often follow.

Moderation produces balance and harmony of *spirit* as well as body. Thomas Aquinas taught that the second encompassing meaning of this virtue is serenity. His understanding seems very modern because today, medicine and psychology have documented that an individual's lifestyle has a great deal to do with that person's physical and psychological health. Illness, physical or mental, can be a result of long-term indulgence and lack of self-discipline.

Historically, Jewish teaching has always affirmed the surpassing importance of the disciplined life. King Solomon in the Book of Proverbs affirms, "[Better is] one whose spirit is controlled than one who captures a city." One of Judaism's greatest contributions in this respect is the Ten Commandments, handed down from God to the people of Israel by Moses. For thousands of years the commandments have been beacons to right living.

Christianity extended the focus of the life of balanced moderation to include a spiritual imperative and dimension: for the Christian, human impulses, affections, and pleasures are disciplined to enable the believer to be free to keep the love of God and others as a primary center in life.

Poets seldom write poems about moderation. They seem more inspired to reflect on humankind's excesses, foibles, and ruinous ambitions and emotions. But poets do celebrate the serene pleasures of a balanced life, the value of humility, and the inner harmony that to the Greeks was the hallmark of the virtue of moderation. An unknown poet has written, "Content I live, this is my stay, I seek no more than may suffice . . . Lo, thus I triumph like a king, Content with that my mind doth bring."

In Praise of a Contented Mind

My mind to me a kingdom is;
Such perfect joy therein I find
That it exceeds all other bliss
That world affords or grows by kind.
Though much I want which most men
    have,
Yet still my mind forbids to crave.

No princely pomp, no wealthy store,
No force to win the victory,
No wily wit to salve a sore,
No shape to feed each grazing eye;
To none of these I yield as thrall.
For why my mind doth serve for all.

I see how plenty suffers oft,
How hasty climbers soon do fall;
I see that those that are aloft
Mishap doeth threaten most of all;
They get with toil, they keep with fear.
Such cares my mind could never bear.

Content I live, this is my stay;
I seek no more than may suffice;
I press to bear no haughty sway;
Look what I lack my mind supplies;
Lo, thus I triumph like a king,
Content with that my mind doth bring.

Some have too much, yet still do crave;
I little have, and seek no more.
They are but poor, though much they
    have,
And I am rich with little store.
They poor, I rich; they beg, I give;
They lack, I leave; they pine, I live.

I laugh not at another's loss;
I grudge not at another's gain;
No worldly waves my mind can toss;
My state at one doth still remain.
I fear no foe, nor fawning friend;
I loathe not life, nor dread my end.

Some weigh their pleasure by their lust,
Their wisdom by their rage of will,
Their treasure is their only trust;
And cloaked craft their store of skill.
But all the pleasure that I find
Is to maintain a quiet mind.

My wealth is health and perfect ease;
My conscience clear my chief defense;
I neither seek by bribes to please,
Nor by deceit to breed offence.
Thus do I live; thus will I die.
Would all did so as well as I!

—ANONYMOUS

Serenity

Here's a sigh for those who love me
And a smile to those who hate;
And whatever sky's above me,
Here's a heart for every fate.

—LORD BYRON

Proportion

It is better to live a short life of balance and beauty than a long life that is shrunken and empty.

It is not growing like a tree
In bulk, doth make man better be;
Or standing long an oak, three hundred
   year,
To fall a log at last, dry, bald, and sear[1];
A lily of a day,
Is fairer far, in May,
Although it fall, and die that night,
It was the plant and flower of Light.
In small proportions, we just beauties see;
In short measures, life may perfect be.

—BEN JONSON

[1] Withered

Moderation

Neither impulsiveness nor resistance to change are marks of a reasoned person.

Be not the first by whom the new are
   tried.
Nor yet the last to lay the old aside.

   —ALEXANDER POPE

In a Child's Album

Small service is true service while it lasts;
Of humblest friends, bright creature! Scorn
   not one;
The Daisy, by the shadow that it casts,
Protects the lingering dew-drop from the
   sun.

—WILLIAM WORDSWORTH

Four Things

Four things a man must learn to do
If he would make his record true:
To think without confusion clearly;
To love his fellowmen sincerely;
To act from honest motives purely;
To trust in God and Heaven securely.

—HENRY VAN DYKE

True Rest

Rest is not quitting
The busy career;
Rest is the fitting
Of self to one's sphere.

'Tis the brook's motion
Clear without strife,
Fleeing to ocean,
After this life.

'Tis loving and serving,
The highest and best;
'Tis onward, unswerving,
And this is true rest.

—JOHANN WOLFGANG VON GOETHE

A Little Work

A little work, a little play
To keep us going—and so, good-day!

A little warmth, a little light
Of love's bestowing—and so, good-night!

A little fun, to match the sorrow
Of each day's growing—and so, good-
    morrow.

A little trust that when we die
We reap our sowing! And so—good-bye!

—GEORGE DU MAURIER

The Shepherd Boy's Song

He that is down needs fear no fall,
He that is low, no pride;
He that is humble ever shall
Have God to be his guide.

I am content with what I have,
Little it be or much:
And, Lord, contentment still I crave,
Because Thou savest such.

Fullness to such a burden is
That go on pilgrimage:
Here little, and hereafter bliss,
Is best from age to age.

—JOHN BUNYAN

Anger

Anger in its time and place,
May assume a kind of grace.
It must have some reason in it,
And not last beyond a minute.
If to further lengths it go,
It does into malice grow.
'Tis the difference we can see
'Twixt the serpent and the bee.
If the latter you provoke,
It inflicts a hasty stroke,
Put you to some little pain,
But it *never stings again.*
Close in tufted bush or brake
Lurks the poison-swelled snake
Nursing up his cherished wrath;
In the purlieus[1] of his path,
In the cold, or in the warm,
Mean him good, or mean him harm,
Wheresoever fate may bring you
The vile snake *will always sting you.*

—CHARLES and MARY LAMB

[1] Places that one goes often

Temper My Intemperance

Temper my intemperance, O Lord,
O hallowed, O adored,
My heart's creator, mighty, wild,
Temper Thy bewildered child.
Blaze my eye and blast my ear,
Let me never fear to fear
Nor forget what I have heard,
Even your voice, my Lord.
Even your Word.

—MADELEINE L'ENGLE

The Gift

Robert Burns wrote in his Scottish Highland dialect, which gives a whimsical touch to his words. He says if we could see ourselves as other people see us, we would give up our affectations of dress, walk, and even the mannered way we pray.

O wad[1] some Pow'r the giftie gie[2] us
To see ourselves as ithers see us!
It wad frae[3] mony[4] a blunder free us,
And foolish notion:
What airs[5] in dress and gait[6] wad lea'e
   us[7]
And ev'n devotion!

   —ROBERT BURNS

[1] Would
[2] Give
[3] From
[4] Many
[5] Vanity
[6] A way of walking or stepping
[7] Would leave us

A Poison Tree

Blake describes the importance of simplicity and directness in human relationships. If one retains anger and allows it to grow, it becomes murderous.

I was angry with my friend:
I told my wrath, my wrath did end.
I was angry with my foe:
I told it not, my wrath did grow.

And I watered it in fears,
Night and morning with my tears;
And I sunned it with smiles,
And with soft, deceitful wiles.

And it grew both day and night,
Till it bore an apple bright;
And my foe beheld it shine,
And he knew that it was mine.

And into my garden stole,
When the night had veiled the pole:
In the morning glad I see
My foe outstretched beneath the tree.

—WILLIAM BLAKE

Moderation in the Bible

Athletes exercise self-control in all things; they do it to receive a perishable wreath, but we an imperishable one.

—I Corinthians 9:25

The fruit of the Spirit is love, joy, peace, patience, kindness, generosity, faithfulness, gentleness, and self-control. There is no law against such things.

—Galatians 5:23

Now an overseer must be above reproach, married only once, temperate, sensible, respectable, hospitable, an apt teacher, not a drunkard, not violent but gentle, not quarrelsome, and not a lover of money.

—I Timothy 3:2

You must make every effort to support your faith with goodness, and goodness with knowledge, and knowledge with self-control, and self-control with endurance, and endurance with godliness, and godliness with mutual affection and mutual affection, with love.

—II Peter 1:5–7

For the grace of God has appeared . . . training us . . . to live lives that are self-controlled, upright, and godly . . .

—Titus 2:11–12

Forbearance

Hast thou named all the birds without a
   gun?
Loved the wood-rose, and left it on its
   stalk?
At rich men's tables eaten bread and
   pulse[1]?
Unarmed, faced danger with a heart of
   trust?
And loved so well a high behavior,
In man or maid, that thou from speech
   refrained,
Nobility, more nobly to repay?
O, be my friend, and teach me to be
   thine!

—RALPH WALDO EMERSON

[1] Peas and beans—simple vegetables

Example

Like the star
Shining afar
Slowly now
And without rest,
Let each man turn, with steady sway,
Round the task that rules the day
And do his best.

—Johann Wolfgang von Goethe

A Thanksgiving to God for His House

Often it is life's simple blessings, easily over-looked, that we are most thankful for.

Lord, thou has given me a cell
    Wherein to dwell,
A little house, whose humble roof
    Is weather-proof,
Under the spars[1] of which I lie
    Both soft and dry;
Where thou, my chamber for to ward,
    Has set a guard
Of humble thoughts to watch and keep
    Me, while I sleep.
Low is my porch, as is my fate,
    Both void of state;
And yet the threshold of my door
    Is worn by th' poor,
Who thither come and freely get
    Good words, or meat.
Like as my parlor, so my hall
    And kitchen small;

[1] Strong beams

A little buttery[2], and therein
    A little bin,
Which keeps my little loaf of bread
    Unchipped, unfleaed;
Some brittle sticks of thorn or briar
    Make me a fire,
Close by whose living coal I sit,
    And glow like it.
Lord, I confess, too, when I dine,
    The pulse[3] is thine,
And all those other bits that be
    There placed by thee;
The worts, the purslain, and the mess[4]
    Of water-cress,
Which of thy kindness thou hast sent;
    And my content
Makes those, and my beloved beet,
    To be more sweet.
'Tis thou that crown'st my glittering hearth
    with guiltless mirth,

[2] Pantry
[3] Edible seeds of plants: beans, lentils
[4] The plants, the vegetables, and the quantity of food sufficient for a dish

And giv'st me wassail[5] bowls to drink,
  spiced to the brink.
Lord, 'tis thy plenty-dropping hand
  That soils my land,
And giv'st me, for my bushel sown,
  Twice ten for one;
Thou mak'st my teeming hen to lay
  Her egg each day;
Besides my healthful ewes to bear
  Me twins each year;
The while the conduits of my kine[6]
  Run cream, for wine.

All these, and better thou doest send
  Me, to this end,
That I should render, for my part,
  A thankful heart,
Which, fired with incense, I resign,
  As wholly thine;
But the acceptance, that must be,
  My Christ, by thee.

—ROBERT HERRICK

[5] Spiced ale
[6] Cows

Ode on Solitude

Happy the man whose wish and care
A few paternal acres bound,
Content to breathe his native air,
    In his own ground.

Whose herds with milk, whose fields with
   bread,
Whose flocks supply him with attire,
Whose trees in summer yield him shade,
    In winter fire.

Blest, who can unconcern'dly find
Hours, days, and years slide soft away,
In health of body, peace of mind,
    Quiet by day.

Sound sleep by night; study and ease,
Together mixt; sweet recreation;
And Innocence, which most does please
    With meditation.

Thus let me live, unseen, unknown,
Thus unlamented, let me die,
Steal from the world, and not a stone
        Tell where I lie.

—ALEXANDER POPE

from *Endymion*[1]

On dark days, admiring something beautiful can lift our spirits and restore us to a balanced perspective.

A thing of beauty is a joy forever:
Its loveliness increases; it will never
Pass into nothingness; but still will keep
A bower quiet for us, and a sleep
Full of sweet dreams, and health, and
    quiet breathing.
Therefore, on every morrow, are we
    wreathing
A flowery band to bind us to the earth,
Spite of despondence, of the inhuman
    dearth
Of noble natures, of the gloomy days,
Of all the unhealthy and o'er-darkened
    ways
Made for our searching: yes, in spite of
    all,

---

[1] In Greek mythology, Endymion was a handsome youth who was loved by a moon goddess and who was preserved by eternal sleep.

Some shape of beauty moves away the
  pall
From our dark spirits.

—JOHN KEATS

Moderation is not a negation of intensity, but helps avoid monotony

Will you stop for a while, stop trying to
    pull yourself together
for some clear "meaning"—some
    momentary summary?
    no one
can have poetry or dances, prayers or
    climaxes all day;
    the ordinary
blankness of little dramatic consciousness
    is good for the health sometimes,
only Dostoyevsky can be Dostoyevskian at
    such long tumultuous stretches;
look what intensity did to poor great Van
    Gogh!;
    linger, lunge,
Scrounge and be stupid, that doesn't take
    much centering of one's forces;
as wise Whitman said, "lounge and invite
    the soul." Get enough sleep;
and not only because (as Cocteau said)
    "poetry is the literature of sleep";

be a dumb bell for a few minutes at least;
   we don't want
   Sunday church bells
   ringing constantly.

—JOHN TAGLIABUE

Moderation

This ancient poem speaks of the danger of excessive ambition.

Not in *every* generation do virtues long-
    descended
Breed men of might. Not *always* do the
    black fields bounteously
Give harvest; not with *every* summer
    ended
Like wealth will load the fragrant
    blossomed tree;
But with changeful alteration. So too for
    humanity

Fate stands. What God's disposal shall
    ordain us,
No token tells. And yet we launch out
    evermore
On perilous quests—our wanton hopes
    enchain us—
The tides of foresight lie beyond our lore.

Keep measure in ambition. Sharp the pain
Of mad hearts craving what no hand shall
  gain.

—Pindar of Thebes

From Hamlet's Advice to the Players

Hamlet's counsel, addressed to actors, and written over four hundred years ago, is still good advice for conversation today.

Speak the speech, I pray you as I
    pronounc'd it to you, trippingly on the
    tongue;
but if you mouth it, as many of our players
    do, I had as lief the town-crier spoke
    my lines.
Nor do not saw the air too much with your
    hand, thus, but use all gently;
for in the very torrent, tempest, and, as I
    may say, whirlwind of your passion,
you must acquire and beget a temperance
    that may give it smoothness.

Be not too tame neither, but let your own
   discretion be your tutor.
Suit the action to the word, the word to
   the action; with this special observance,
that you o'erstep not the modesty of
   nature;

—WILLIAM SHAKESPEARE,
   Hamlet, Act 3, Scene 2

Of Moderation and Tolerance

He that has grown to wisdom hurries not,
But thinks and weighs what Reason bids
  him do
And after thinking he retains his thought
Until as he conceived the fact ensue.
Let no man to o'erweening pride be
  wrought,
But count his state as Fortune's gift and
  due.
He is a fool who deems that none has
  sought
The truth, save he alone, or knows it true.
Many strange birds are on the air abroad,
Nor all are of one flight or of one force,
But each after his kind dissimilar:
To each was portioned of the breath of
  God,
Who gave them divers instincts from one
  source.
Then judge not thou thy fellows what they
  are.

   —GUIDO GUINICELLI,
      translated by D. G. Rossetti

FAITH

THE WORD "FAITH" is commonly used in America today. We say, "Thanks for your faith in me," or "I have no faith in that product," or "We've got to have faith that everything will work out all right." The cardinal virtue faith is very different from these ordinary ways of using the word. It towers above human expressions of trust as the first of the three great theological virtues: faith, hope, and love. These virtues are called "theological" because they don't arise from Greek philosophy, but from the biblical writings of the New Testament. Faith, hope, and love also have a second distinction—they are considered "graces" as well as virtues because they cannot be attained by human determination and effort. They are gifts from God.

When the events described in the New Testament were taking place, the only real "faith" in the Roman world was faith in the military power of Rome. People didn't take seriously the mythic gods of the Greco-Roman culture or have much belief in the declaration that Caesar was a god. Superstition, magic, and mystery religions were in vogue. Faith was as casual, intellectualized, easily changed, and unfocused as it can often seem today.

The Apostle Paul wrote powerfully about faith in God. His position, although respectful of people's pagan searchings, went something like, "Never mind trying out this idea and then another one, always looking around for something better or more interesting to explore. That isn't faith. Faith is commitment to the One, True God." Paul would have agreed that having faith is a commitment like getting married as compared to just telling someone you will love them forever. It is diving into the lake for a swim rather than sitting on the beach and discussing the merits of exercise. One of Paul's great contributions to Christianity is his understanding that faith is an attitude of the entire self. Faith involves not only belief in God; it must also include a resolve to act out one's faith in godly living. This kind of commitment concept is what the cardinal virtue faith entails.

Paul's focus on faith sprang from his Hebrew roots. Judaism's approach to faith was a certainty based on God's promises to the Jewish people, and their response of obedience to God's laws. For Paul and the other New Testament writers, faith's center was in a person's relationship to Jesus Christ. These writers were very clear that faith is documented in how a person lives, not by what that person professes at any given moment. This concept might have been mildly alarming to people in New Testament times and perhaps it still is today. The idea that faith only exists if it is wholeheartedly practiced can be disconcerting.

Christianity maintains that the virtue of faith profoundly changes the quality of life. From faith flows the assurance that the universe is not empty: God inhabits, and is beyond, creation. God sees each human life, and approves and rewards faith. Emily Dickinson has expressed the godly trust of generations with her lines, ''I never spoke with God, Nor visited in Heaven—Yet certain am I of the spot As if the Checks were given.''

(I Never Saw a Moor)

I never saw a Moor—
I never saw the Sea—
Yet I know how the Heather looks
And what a Billow[1] be.

I never spoke with God
Nor visited in Heaven—
Yet certain am I of the spot
As if the Checks were given—

—EMILY DICKINSON

[1] A large wave or swell of the sea

Who Has Seen the Wind?

Who has seen the wind?
Neither I nor you:
But when the leaves hang trembling,
The wind is passing through.

Who has seen the wind?
Neither you nor I:
But when the trees bow down their heads,
The wind is passing by.

—CHRISTINA ROSSETTI

The Year's at the Spring

The year's at the spring,
And day's at the morn;
Morning's at seven;
The hill-side's dew-pearled;
The lark's on the wing;
The snail's on the thorn:
God's in His heaven—
All's right with the world.

—ROBERT BROWNING

The Shepherd

How sweet is the shepherd's sweet lot;
From the morn to the evening he strays;
He shall follow his sheep all the day,
And his tongue shall be filled with praise.

For he hears the lamb's innocent call,
And he hears the ewe's tender reply;
He is watchful while they are at peace,
For they know when their shepherd is
  nigh.

—WILLIAM BLAKE

Faith

If a wren can cling
To a spray a-swing
In the mad May winds, and sing and sing,
And if she's burst for joy;
Why cannot I
Contented lie
In His quiet arms beneath the sky,
Unmoved by earth's annoy?

—F. B. MEYER

Out in the Fields with God

The little cares which fretted me
I lost them yesterday,
Among the fields, above the sea,
Among the winds at play,
Among the lowing of the herds,
The rustling of the trees,
Among the singing of the birds,
The humming of the bees.
The foolish fear of what might happen,
I cast them all away
Among the clover-scented grass,
Among the new-mown hay,
Among the husking of the corn,
Where drowsy poppies nod
Where ill thoughts die and good are
    born—
Out in the fields with God.

—ELIZABETH BARRETT BROWNING

Lamps

O I am all for little lamps
When the shadows fall,
Blue and gold and crimson lamps,
Squatty, plump, or tall,

Curving crystal chimneys
With bumpy crocheted brims,
Or a thin sheath of fine glass
That rounds and curves and slims.

O I am all for little lamps
When the shadows loom,
Little, dusty, golden lamps,
Shining through the gloom.

Swinging crimson lanterns
When my heart would roam,
And bending finger-tips of flame
Beckoning me home.

And for windy, wild nights,
Street-lamps, shadow-rimmed,
And little rosy, cosy lamps
By couches, deep and dimmed.

And Oh, I love a white lamp
When the cloth is spread,
Shining on the yellow cream
And the snowy bread.

And tiny sparks of silver
Twinkling in the night,
Or lamps as soft as twined flame
That kiss old eyes with light.

O I have need of cottage lamps
To make the shadows roll,
With the little lamps of heaven
To guide my stumbling soul.

—KATHLEEN DAVIDSON

Psalm 23

The Lord is my shepherd; I shall not want.

He maketh me to lie down in green pastures: he leadeth me beside the still waters.

He restoreth my soul: he leadeth me in the paths of righteousness for his name's sake.

Yea, though I walk through the valley of the shadow of death, I will fear no evil: for thou art with me; thy rod and thy staff they comfort me.

Thou preparest a table before me in the presence of mine enemies: thou anointest my head with oil; my cup runneth over.

Surely goodness and mercy shall follow me all the days of my life: and I will dwell in the house of the Lord for ever.

(KJV)

Let Us with a Gladsome Mind

Let us with a gladsome mind
Praise the Lord for He is kind;
For His mercies aye endure,
Ever faithful, ever sure.

Let us blaze His name abroad,
For of gods He is the God;
Who by all-commanding might,
Filled the new-made world with light.

He the golden tressed sun
Caused all day his course to run;
Th' horned moon to shine by night,
'Mid her spangled sisters bright.

He His chosen race did bless,
In the wasteful wilderness;
He hath, with a piteous eye,
Looked upon our misery.

All things living He doth feed,
His full hand supplies their need;
For His mercies aye endure,
Ever faithful, ever sure.

—JOHN MILTON

i thank You God for most
this amazing

i thank You God for most this amazing
day: for the leaping greenly spirits of trees
and a blue true dream of sky; and for
  everything
which is natural which is infinite which is
  yes

(i who have died am alive again today,
and this is the sun's birthday; this is the
  birth
day of life and of love and wings: and of
  the gay
great happening illimitably[1] earth)

how should tasting touching hearing
  seeing
breathing any—lifted from the no
of all nothing—human merely being
doubt unimaginable You?

[1] Incapable of being limited

209

(now the ears of my ears awake and
now the eyes of my eyes are opened)

—E E CUMMINGS

Faith

Faith is not merely praying
Upon your knees at night;
Faith is not merely staying
Through darkness to the light.

Faith is not merely waiting
For glory that will be,
Faith is not merely hating
The sinful ecstasy.

Faith is the brave endeavor
The splendid enterprise,
The strength to serve, whatever
Conditions may arise.

—S. E. KISER

Faith in the Bible

The righteous live by their faith.

—Habakkuk 2:4

So faith comes from what is heard, and what is heard comes through the word of Christ.

—Romans 10:17

What good is it, my brothers and sisters, if you say you have faith but do not have works? Can faith save you? If a brother or sister is naked and lacks daily food, and one of you says to them, "Go in peace; keep warm and eat your fill," and yet you do not supply their bodily needs, what is the good of that? So faith by itself, if it has no works, is dead.

—James 2:14–17

Now faith is the assurance of things hoped for, the conviction of things not seen.

Indeed, by faith our ancestors received approval.

By faith we understand that the worlds were prepared by the word of God, so that what is seen was made from things that are not visible.

And without faith it is impossible to please God, for whoever would approach him must believe that he exists and that he rewards those who seek him.

—Hebrews, 11:1–3, 6

Child Do Not Throw This Book About

Hilaire Belloc was the father of five children.
His gentle poem captures the innocence of
childhood faith.

Child! do not throw this book about;
    Refrain from that unholy pleasure
Of cutting all the pictures out!
    Preserve it as your chiefest treasure.

Child, have you never heard it said
    That you are heir to all the ages?
Why, then, your hands were never made
    To tear these beautiful thick pages!

Your little hands were made to take
    The better things, and leave the worse
    ones.
They also may be used to shake
    The massive Paws of Elder Persons.

And when your prayers complete the day
   Darling, your little tiny hands
Were also made, I think, to pray
   For men that lose their fairylands.

   —HILAIRE BELLOC

(Lines written on a bookmark found in her prayerbook)

These lines written by St. Teresa in the six-teenth century can beautifully quiet our con-temporary anxieties and never-satisfied needs.

> Let nothing disturb thee,
> Nothing affright thee;
> All things are passing;
> God never changeth;
> Patient endurance
> Attaineth to all things;
> Who God possesseth
> Is nothing wanting;
> Alone God sufficeth.
>
> —TERESA OF ÁVILA

Yom Kippur[1]

To Thee we give ourselves today,
Forgetful of the world outside;
We tarry in Thy house, O Lord,
From eventide to eventide.

From Thy all-searching, righteous eye
Our deepest heart can nothing hide;
It crieth up to Thee for peace
From eventide to eventide.

Who could endure, should'st Thou, O
  God,
As we deserve, forever chide!
We therefore seek Thy pardoning grace
From eventide to eventide.

O may we lay to heart how swift
The years of life do onward glide;
So learn to live that we may see
Thy light at our life's eventide.

—RABBI GUSTAV GOTTHEIL

[1] The Jewish Day of Atonement

St. Patrick's Breastplate (Lorica)

This fifth-century Irish hymn was composed by St. Patrick to protect himself against the Celtic pagan priests who sought to kill him.

I arise to-day
    through a mighty strength, the
    invocation of the Trinity,
    through belief in the Threeness,
    through confession of the Oneness
    toward the Creator.

I arise today
    through the strength of Christ with His
        Baptism,
    through the strength of His Crucifixion
        with His Burial,
    through the strength of His Resurrection
        with His Ascension,
    through the strength of His descent for
        the Judgement of Doom.

I arise today
    through the strength of the love of
        Cherubim,
    in obedience of Angels,
    in the service of the Archangels,
    in hope of resurrection to meet with
        reward,
    in prayers of the Prophets,
    in preachings of Apostles,
    in faiths of Confessors,
    in innocence of Holy Virgins,
    in deeds of righteous men.

I arise today
    through the strength of Heaven:
    light of the Sun,
    brilliance of the Moon,
    splendor of Fire,
    speed of Lightning,
    swiftness of Wind
    depth of Sea,
    stability of Earth,
    firmness of Rock.

I arise today
    through God's strength to pilot me:
    God's might to uphold me,
    God's wisdom to guide me,
    God's eye to look before me,
    God's ear to hear me,
    God's word to speak for me,
    God's hand to guard me,
    God's way to lie before me,
    God's shield to protect me—
        against snares of devils,
        against temptations of vices,
        against inclinations of nature,
        against everyone who shall wish me
          ill,
        afar and near,
        alone and in a crowd.

Christ protect me today
	against poison, against burning,
	against drowning, against wounding,
	so that there may come abundance of
	reward.
Christ with me, Christ before me, Christ
	behind me,
Christ in me, Christ beneath me, Christ
	above me,
Christ on my right, Christ on my left,
Christ where I lie, Christ where I sit, Christ
	where I arise,
Christ in the heart of every man who
	thinks of me,
Christ in the mouth of every man who
	speaks to me,
Christ in every eye that sees me,
Christ in every ear that hears me.

I arise today
	through a mighty strength, the
	invocation of the Trinity,
	through belief in Threeness,
	through confession of the Oneness
	towards the Creator.

Salvation is of the Lord.
Salvation is of the Lord.
Salvation is of the Lord.
May Thy salvation, O Lord, be ever with
us.

—St. Patrick, translated by
W. Stokes and J. Strachan

Evensong

The embers of the day are red
Beyond the murky hill.
The kitchen smokes; the bed
In the darkling house is spread:
The great sky darkens overhead,
And the great woods are shrill.
So far have I been led,
Lord, by Thy will:
So far I have followed, Lord, and
    wondered still.
The breeze from the embalmed land
Blows sudden towards the shore,
And claps my cottage door.
I hear the signal, Lord—I understand.
The night at Thy command
Comes. I will eat and sleep and will not
    question more.

—ROBERT LOUIS STEVENSON

Prayer

Pray for my soul. More things are wrought
   by prayer
Than this world dreams of. Wherefore let
   thy voice
Rise like a fountain for me night and day.
For what are men better than sheep or
   goats
That nourish a blind life within the brain,
If, knowing God, they lift not hands of
   prayer
Both for themselves and those who call
   them friends?
For so the whole round earth is every way
Bound by gold chains about the feet of
   God.

—ALFRED LORD TENNYSON

Faith

O never star
Was lost; here
We all aspire to heaven and there is
  heaven
Above us.
If I stoop
Into a dark tremendous sea of cloud,
It is but for a time; I press God's lamp
Close to my breast; its splendor soon or
  late
Will pierce the gloom. I shall emerge some
  day.

—ROBERT BROWNING

Psalm 121

I will lift up mine eyes unto the hills, from
whence cometh my help.
My help cometh from the Lord, which made
heaven and earth.
He will not suffer thy foot to be moved: he
that keepeth thee will not slumber.
Behold, He that keepeth Israel shall neither
slumber nor sleep.
The Lord is thy keeper: the Lord is thy
shade upon thy right hand.
The sun shall not smite thee by day, nor the
moon by night.
The Lord shall preserve thee from all evil: he
shall preserve thy soul.
The Lord shall preserve thy going out and
thy coming in from this time forth, and
even for evermore.

(KJV)

Consider

Rossetti bases her poem on Christ's words: "Do not be anxious for your life . . . look at the birds of the air . . . the lilies of the field . . . Will not God do much more for you?" (Matthew 6:26, 28, 30)

Consider
The lilies of the field, whose bloom is
   brief—
     We are as they;
     Like them we fade away,
       As doth a leaf.

Consider
The sparrows of the air, of small account:
     Our God doth view
     Whether they fall or mount—
       He guards us too.

Consider
The lilies, that do neither spin nor toil,
  Yet are most fair—
  What profits all this care,
    And all this coil?[1]

Consider
The birds that have no barn nor harvest-
  weeks:
  God gives them food—
  Much more our Father seeks
    To do us good.

—CHRISTINA ROSSETTI

[1] Disturbance or fuss

Thankfulness

You gave me gifts, God-Enchanter.
I give you thanks for good and ill.
Eternal light in everything on earth.
As now, so on the day after my death.

—Czeslaw Milosz

Up-Hill

Many poets describe the life of faith as a challenging journey. In this question-and-answer poem, the traveler is reassured.

Does the road wind up-hill all the way?
   Yes, to the very end.
Will the day's journey take the whole long
   day?
   From morn to night, my friend.

But is there for the night a resting-place?
   A roof for when the slow dark hours
   begin.
May not the darkness hide it from my
   face?
   You cannot miss that inn.

Shall I meet other wayfarers at night?
   Those who have gone before.
Then must I knock, or call when just in
   sight?
   They will not keep you standing at that
   door.

Shall I find comfort, travel-sore and weak?
  Of labor you shall find the sum.
Will there be beds for me and all who
  seek?
  Yea, beds for all who come.

—CHRISTINA ROSSETTI

Suspended

I had grasped God's garment in the void
but my hand slipped
on the rich silk of it
The "everlasting arms" my sister loved to
   remember
must have upheld my leaden weight
from falling, even so,
for though I claw at empty air and feel
nothing, no embrace,
I have not plummetted.

   —DENISE LEVERTOV

I Would Not Always Reason

I would not always reason. The straight
   path
Wearies us with the never-varying lines,
And we grow melancholy. I would make
Reason my guide, but she should
   sometimes sit
Patiently by the wayside, while I trace
The mazes of pleasant wilderness
Around me. She should be my counselor,
But not my tyrant. For the spirit needs
Impulses from a deeper source than hers;
And there are notions, in the mind of man,
That she must look upon with awe.

—WILLIAM CULLEN BRYANT

Sunday School, Circa 1950

"Who made you?" was always
The question
The answer was always
"God."
Well, there we stood
Three feet high
Heads bowed
Leaning into
Bosoms.

Now
I no longer recall
The Catechism
Or brood on the Genesis
Of life
No.

I ponder the exchange
Itself
And salvage mostly
The leaning.

    —ALICE WALKER

Brotherhood
Homage to Claudius Ptolemy[1]

The poet sees what the astronomer did not: beyond what can be learned from the stars is a Being that has created both stars and humankind.

I am a man: little do I last
and the night is enormous.
But I look up:
the stars write.
Unknowing I understand:
I too am written,
and at this very moment
someone spells me out.

—OCTAVIO PAZ, translated by
Octavio Paz and Eliot Weinberger

---

[1] Ptolemy was a second-century astronomer who studied the motions of the Sun, Moon and planets.

To the Holy Spirit

O Thou, far off and here, whole and
   broken,
Who in necessity and in bounty wait,
Whose truth is light and dark, mute
   though spoken,
By Thy wide grace show me Thy narrow
   gate.

—WENDELL BERRY

You Are

You are the deep epitome of things
that keeps its being secret with locked
   lips,
and shows itself to others otherwise:
to the ship, a haven—to the land, a ship.

—Rainer Maria Rilke

God's Grandeur

The world is charged with the grandeur of
    God.
    It will flame out, like shining from
    shook foil;
    It gathers to a greatness, like the
    ooze of oil[1]
Crushed. Why do men then now not reck
    his rod[2]?
Generations have trod, have trod, have
    trod;
    And all is seared with trade; bleared,
    smeared with toil;
    And wears man's smudge and shares
    man's smell: the soil
Is bare now, nor can foot feel, being shod.
And for all this, nature is never spent;
    There lives the dearest freshness
    deep down things;

[1] Olive oil
[2] Pay attention to his command

And though the last lights off the black
  West went
    Oh, morning, at the brown brink
eastward, springs—
Because the Holy Ghost over the bent
    World broods with warm breast and
with ah! bright wings.

—GERARD MANLEY HOPKINS

The Tide of Faith

So faith is strong
Only when we are strong, shrinks when
  we shrink.
It comes when music stirs us, and the
  chords,
Moving on some grand climax, shakes our
  souls
With influx new that makes new energies.
It comes in swellings of the heart and
  tears
That rise at noble and at gentle deeds.
It comes in moments of heroic love,
Unjealous joy in joy not made for us;
In conscious triumph of the good within,
Making us worship goodness that
  rebukes.
Even our failures are a prophecy,
Even our yearnings and our bitter tears
After that fair and true we cannot grasp.
Presentiment of better things on earth
Sweeps in with every force that stirs our
  souls
To admiration, self-renouncing love.

—GEORGE ELIOT

E Tenebris[1]

Come down, O Christ, and help me!
  Reach thy hand
For I am drowning in a stormier sea
Than Simon on thy lake of Galilee:
The wine of life is spilt upon the sand,
My heart is as some famine-murdered
  land
When all good things have perished
  utterly,
And well I know my soul in Hell must lie
If I this night before God's throne should
  stand.
"He sleeps, perchance, or rideth to the
  chase,
Like Baal, when his prophets howled the
  name

[1] Out of the darkness

From morn till noon on Carmel's smitten
    height.[2]
Nay, peace, I shall behold before the
    night,
The feet of brass,[3] the robe more white
    than flame,
The wounded hands, the weary human
    face.

—OSCAR WILDE

[2] In I Kings 18:27 the prophets of the idol Baal meet Elijah on Mount Carmel for a contest between Baal and God. The false prophets frantically call on Baal, but he is silent. Elijah mocks them by suggesting that perhaps their Baal is asleep or traveling. In the poem, the poet fears at first that God will be silent, but then anticipates a vision of Christ.

[3] In the Apostle John's vision of Christ in the Revelation, St. John describes Christ's feet as shining like polished brass.

The Lamb

The lamb is a traditional symbol of innocence and purity; in Christian tradition, it is also a symbol of Christ, the Agnes Dei, *the Lamb of God.*

Little lamb, who made thee?
Dost thou know who made thee?
Gave thee life, and bid thee feed,
By the streams and o'er the mead;
Gave thee clothing of delight,
Softest clothing, wooly, bright;
Gave thee such a tender voice,
Making all the vales rejoice!
   Little lamb, who made thee?
   Dost thou know who made thee?

Little lamb, I'll tell thee,
Little lamb, I'll tell thee!
He is called by thy name,
For He calls Himself a Lamb:
He is meek and He is mild,
He became a little child:
I a child and thou a lamb,
We are called by his name.
Little lamb, God bless thee.
Little lamb, God bless thee.

—WILLIAM BLAKE

A Hymn to God the Father

*John Donne's last name (pronounced "done")
is used creatively in this early seventeenth-
century poem for forgiveness.*

Wilt Thou forgive that sin, where I begun,
Which was my sin, though it were done
  before?
Wilt Thou forgive that sin; through which I
  run,
And do run still: though still I do deplore?
When Thou hast done, Thou hast not
  done,
       For I have more.

Wilt Thou forgive that sin which I have
  won
Others to sin? And, made my sin their
  door?
Wilt Thou forgive that sin which I did shun
A year or two: but wallowed in, a score?
When Thou hast done, Thou hast not
  done,
       For I have more.

I have a sin of fear, that when I have spun
My last thread, I shall perish on the shore;
But swear by Thyself, that at my death
   Thy Son
Shall shine as He shines now, and
   heretofore;
And, having done that, Thou hast done,
      I fear no more.

—JOHN DONNE

Where Goest Thou?

You say, "Where goest thou?" I cannot
   tell,
And still go on. If but the way be straight
I cannot go amiss: before me lies
Dawn and the day: the night behind me:
   that
Suffices me: I break the bounds: I see,
And nothing more; believe and nothing
   less.
My future is not one of my concerns.

   —VICTOR HUGO

To a Waterfowl

As the poet watches the solitary flight of the bird, he is reminded that the God who guides the Waterfowl "through the boundless sky" will just as surely guide his own path through life.

Wither midst falling dew,
While glow the heavens with the last
    steps of day,
Far, through their rosy depths, dost thou
    pursue
      Thy solitary way?

Vainly the fowler's[1] eye
Might mark thy distant flight to do thee
    wrong,
As, darkly painted on the crimson sky,
      Thy figure floats along.

[1] A hunter of edible birds

Seek'st thou the plashy brink
Of weedy lake, or marge of river wide,
Or where the rocking billows rise and
　　sink
　　　　On the chafed ocean-side?

　　　　There is a Power whose care
Teaches thy way along that pathless
　　coast—
The desert and illimitable air,—
　　　　Lone wandering, but not lost.

　　　　All day thy wings have fanned,
At that far height, the cold, thin
　　atmosphere,
Yet stoop not, weary, to the welcome
　　land,
　　　　Though the dark night is near.

　　　　And soon that toil shall end;
Soon shalt thou find a summer home,
　　and rest,
And scream among thy fellows; reeds
　　shall bend,
　　　　Soon, o'er thy sheltered nest.

Thou'rt gone, the abyss of
heaven
Hath swallowed up thy form; yet, on my
heart
Deeply hath sunk the lesson thou hast
given,
And shall not soon depart.

He who, from zone to zone,
Guides through the boundless sky thy
certain flight,
In the long way that I must tread alone,
Will lead my steps aright.

—WILLIAM CULLEN BRYANT

Man, Bird, and God

Browning may have been thinking of the words of Jesus to his disciples: "And how much more valuable are you than birds!" (Luke 12:24)

I Go to prove my soul!
I see my way as birds their trackless way.
I shall arrive! what time, what circuit first,
I ask not: but unless God send his hail
Or blinding fireballs, sleet or stifling snow,
In some time, his good time, I shall arrive:
He guides me and the bird. In his good
    time!

—ROBERT BROWNING

Pax

All that matters is to be at one with the
    living God
To be a creature in the house of the God
    of Life.
Like a cat asleep on a chair
At peace, in peace
And at one with the master of the house,
    with the mistress,
At home, at home in the house of the
    living,
Sleeping on the hearth, and yawning
    before the fire.

Sleeping on the hearth of the living world
Yawning at home before the fire of life
Feeling the presence of the living God
Like a great reassurance
A deep calm in the heart
A presence
As of a master sitting at the board
In his own and greater being,
In the house of life.

—D. H. Lawrence

Song of the brightness of water

The deep well reminds the poet of his soul's sadness and emptiness. But the water more deeply reflects the brightness of God's world and His revelation in nature.

From this depth—I came only to draw water
in a jug—so long ago, this brightness
still clings to my eyes—the perception I found,
and so much empty space, my own,
reflected in the well.

Yet it is good. I can never take all of you
into me. Stay then as a mirror in the well.
Leaves and flowers remain, and each astonished gaze
brings them down
to my eyes transfixed more by light
than by sorrow.

—Karol Wojtyla (Pope John Paul II),
translated by Jerzy Peterkiewicz

Answers

Sometimes we busy ourselves with small concerns in order to avoid confronting the great issues of life. Yet the "big answers" press upon us, "shouting to be acknowledged and believed." It is by faith that we accept God's "great conclusions."

I kept my answers small and kept them
   near;
Big questions bruised my mind but still I
   let
Small answers be a bulwark to my fear.

The huge abstractions I kept from the
   light;
Small things I handled and caressed and
   loved.
I let the stars assume the whole of night.

But the big answers clamoured to be
   moved
Into my life. Their great audacity
Shouted to be acknowledged and
   believed.

Even when all small answers build up to
Protection of my spirit, still I hear
Big answers striving for their overthrow

And all the great conclusions coming near.

—E<small>LIZABETH</small> J<small>ENNINGS</small>

You, Neighbor God

You, neighbor God, if sometimes in the
   night
I rouse you with loud knocking, I do so
only because I seldom hear you breathe;
I know: you are alone
And should you need a drink, no one is
   there
to reach it to you, groping in the dark.
Always I hearken. Give but a small sign.
I am quite near.

Between us there is but a narrow wall,
and by sheer chance; for it would take
merely a call from your lips or from mine
to break it down,
and that all noiselessly.

The wall is builded of your images.

They stand before you hiding you like
   names,
And when the light within me blazes high
that in my inmost soul I know you by,
the radiance is squandered on their
   frames.

And then my senses, which too soon grow
    lame,
exiled from, you, must go their homeless
    ways.

—RAINER MARIA RILKE

And Death Shall Have No Dominion

Thomas makes dramatic use of the New Testament phrase "death hath no more dominion over him." (Romans 6:9)

And death shall have no dominion.
Dead men naked they shall be one
With the man in the wind and the west
    moon;
When their bones are picked clean and
    the clean bones gone,
They shall have stars at elbow and foot;
Though they go mad they shall be sane,
Though they sink through the sea they
    shall rise again;
Though lovers be lost love shall not;
And death shall have no dominion.

And death shall have no dominion.
Under the windings of the sea
They lying long shall not die windily;
Twisting on racks when sinews give way,
Strapped to a wheel, yet they shall not
   break;
Faith in their hands shall snap in two,
And the unicorn evils run them through;
Split all ends up they shan't crack;
And death shall have no dominion.

And death shall have no dominion.
No more may gulls cry at their ears
Or waves break loud on the seashores;
Where blew a flower may a flower no
   more
Lift its head to the blows of the rain;
Though they be mad and dead as nails,
Heads of the characters hammer through
   daisies;
Break in the sun till the sun breaks down,
And death shall have no dominion.

   —DYLAN THOMAS

HOPE

IN CONVERSATION we use the word "hope" to express what we expect to happen, or what we wish would happen: we hope the weather will be nice for an outing, we hope traffic will be light for a drive to the airport, we hope the movie will be good. Our hopes tend to be cursory but they can also express intense concern: we hope the baby will recover quickly, we hope we get the job. Sometimes we think of a hopeful person as a cheerful person, a kind of naïve "Pollyanna" who sees only the bright side of life. Many people, however, seldom really hope for anything; they school themselves to accept what comes along, "taking the bad with the good."

Perhaps this is because the twentieth century has been a time characterized more often by despair than by hope. All possible evils seem to have been rained upon our times: wars, disease, famine, poverty, anarchy. Governments and programs that promise solutions often have failed. In such times, human hope falters.

The cardinal virtue, hope, transcends human history and despair because its source is not in this changing world. The Bible's great call to hope is directed beyond what is visible to the invisible. Its perspective soars into the future, shining with the vision of resurrection, a golden age when God's final plan for humankind will be fulfilled, and heaven, ultimately, will be attained. There is assurance and comfort for this world as well: people who have hope in God are promised spiritual security, safety, refuge, and deliverance.

In writing about the three theological virtues of faith, hope, and love, St. Augustine said that without hope, the four ancient "natural virtues" could not be attained. Without hope, for example, what would be the point of people striving to act wisely, do justice, have courage, and live a disciplined life?

Christianity's "blessed hope," as defined in the New Testament, includes the anticipation of Christ's return, and justification before God for those with faith in Christ. Judaism and Islam also anticipate a final victory of good over evil at the end of human history, producing a state of blessedness. Judaism's distinctive hope has always been connected to the return of Israel to its promised land and the coming of the Messiah, who will bring justice and peace. Islam teaches that at the end of time, all of humanity will be given everlasting punishments or rewards according to their deeds on earth.

Some poets write directly about theological hope: resurrection and heaven are common themes. Others write about possibilities of good, new beginnings, the coming near of God, and the almost unexplainable optimism deep within the human heart. Sheenagh Pugh writes, "Sometimes our best efforts do not go amiss; sometimes we do as we were meant to. The sun will sometimes melt a field of sorrow that seemed hard frozen: may it happen for you."

Sometimes

Sometimes things don't go, after all,
from bad to worse. Some years muscadel
faces down frost; green thrives; the crops
    don't fail,
sometimes a man aims high, and all goes
    well.

A people sometimes will step back from
    war;
elect an honest man; decide they care
enough, that they can't leave some
    stranger poor.
Some men become what they were born
    for.

Sometimes our best efforts do not go
amiss; sometimes we do as we were
    meant to.
The sun will sometimes melt a field of
    sorrow
that seemed hard frozen: may it happen
    for you.

—SHEENAGH PUGH

("Hope" Is the Thing with Feathers)

"Hope" is the thing with feathers—
That perches in the soul—
And sings the tunes without the words—
And never stops—at all—

And sweetest—in the Gale—is heard—
And sore must be the storm—
That could abash the little Bird
That kept so many warm—

I've heard it in the chillest land—
And on the strangest Sea—
Yet, never, in Extremity,
It asked a crumb—of Me.

—EMILY DICKINSON

Hope

Hope, like a gleaming taper's light,
Adorns and cheers our way;
And still, as darker grows the night,
Emits a brighter ray.

—OLIVER GOLDSMITH

The Trees

The trees are coming into leaf
Like something almost being said;
The recent buds relax and spread,
Their greenness is a kind of grief.

Is it that they are born again
And we grow old? No, they die too.
Their yearly trick of looking new
Is written down in rings of grain.

Yet still the unresting castles thresh
In fullgrown thickness every May.
Last year is dead, they seem to say,
Begin afresh, afresh, afresh.

—PHILIP LARKIN

from *The Round*

Light splashed this morning
on the shell-pink anemones
swaying on their tall stems;
down blue-spiked veronica
light flowed in rivulets
over the humps of the honeybees;
this morning I saw light kiss
the silk of the roses
in their second flowering,
my late bloomers
flushed with their brandy.
A curious gladness shook me . . .

I can scarcely wait till tomorrow
when a new life begins for me
as it does each day,
as it does each day.

—STANLEY KUNITZ

Crossing the Bar

Sunset and evening star,
And one clear call for me.
And may there be no moaning of the bar[1],
When I put out to sea,

But such a tide as moving seems asleep,
Too full for sound and foam,
When that which drew from out the
   boundless deep
Turns again home.

Twilight and evening bell,
And after that the dark:
And may there be no sadness of farewell,
When I embark;

For tho' from out our bourne of Time and
   Place
The flood may bear me far,
I hope to see my Pilot face to face,
When I have crost the bar.

—ALFRED LORD TENNYSON

[1] A sandbar: the offshore shoal of sand built up by waves or currents. Metaphorically, the barrier between life and death.

Epitaph

The Body
of
Benjamin Franklin
Printer
(Like the cover of an old book
Its contents torn out
And stript of its lettering and gilding)
Lies here, food for worms.
But the work shall not be lost
For it will (as he believed) appear once
more
In a new and more elegant edition
Revised and corrected
by
The Author.

—Benjamin Franklin

Dreams

Hold fast to dreams
For if dreams die
Life is a broken-winged bird
That cannot fly.

Hold fast to dreams
For when dreams go
Life is a barren field
Frozen with snow.

—LANGSTON HUGHES

The Oxen

There is a legend that oxen kneel on Christmas Eve at midnight in honor of the birth of the Christ Child.

Christmas Eve, and twelve of the clock.
"Now they are all on their knees,"
An elder said as we sat in a flock
By the embers in hearthside ease.

We pictured the meek mild creatures
  where
They dwelt in the strawy pen,
Nor did it occur to one of us there
To doubt they were kneeling then.

So fair a fancy few would weave
In these years! Yet, I feel,
If someone said on Christmas Eve,
"Come; see the oxen kneel,

"In the lonely barton[1] by yonder coomb[2]
Our childhood used to know,"
I should go with him in the gloom,
Hoping it might be so.

—THOMAS HARDY

[1] Farmyard
[2] Valley

My Heart Leaps Up

My heart leaps up when I behold
A rainbow in the sky:
So was it when my life began;
So is it now I am a man;
So be it when I shall grow old,
Or let me die!
The Child is father of the Man;
And I could wish my days to be
Bound each to each by natural piety.

—WILLIAM WORDSWORTH

Heaven

This playful poem is reminiscent of Jesus' observation that if the crowds weren't praising Him as they were, the stones would cry out. (Luke 19:40)

Heaven is
The place where
Happiness is
Everywhere.

Animals
And birds sing—
As does
Everything.

To each stone,
"How-do-you-do?"
Stone answers back,
"Well! And you?"

      —LANGSTON HUGHES

For Lianne, Aged One

As far as possible, stay as you are,
with the eye clear and open
and washed clean of fear;
with the skin untracked
by the sad workings of the heart,
lips unskilled in spite.
As far as possible, stay as you are,
the morning's first light
cause enough for joy,
each passing face
judged only by the color of its smile.
As far as possible, stay as you are.
Gaze out at the world
with its mystery and noise,
but refuse all offers to join.
Be backwards in evil,
advanced in love.
As far as possible, stay as you are,
with the upturned face
and the open palm,
with the stumble of faith
and the shout of hope.
For of such is the Kingdom.

—STEVE TURNER

(I Dwell in Possibility)

I dwell in Possibility—
A fairer House than Prose—
More numerous of Windows—
Superior—for Doors—

Of Chambers as the Cedars—
Impregnable of Eye—
And for an Everlasting Roof
The Gambrels[1] of the Sky—

Of Visitors—the fairest—
For Occupation—This—
The spreading wide my narrow Hands
To gather Paradise—

—EMILY DICKINSON

[1] Curved roofs

Hope

Hope means to keep living
amid desperation,
and to keep humming in darkness.
Hoping is knowing that there is love,
it is trust in tomorrow
it is falling asleep
and waking again
when the sun rises.
In the midst of a gale at sea,
it is to discover land.
In the eye of another
it is to see that he understands you.
As long as there is still hope
there will also be prayer.
And God will be holding you
in His hands.

—HENRI NOUWEN

Even Such Is Time

This poem is said to have been written in the Tower of London before Raleigh's execution in 1618.

Even such is time that takes in trust
Our youth, our joys, our all we have,
And pays us but with age and dust,
Who in the dark and silent grave,
When we have wandered all our ways,
Shuts up the story of our days.
But from this earth, this grave, this dust,
My God shall raise me up, I trust.

—Sir Walter Raleigh

When I Heard the Learn'd Astronomer

Even the highest of human learning is inade-quate to explain the wonder of creation. An as-tronomer's classroom lecture on the cosmos is dry and uninspiring. The poet slips away and is restored as he views the mystical and starry night sky "in perfect silence."

When I heard the learn'd astronomer,
When the proofs, the figures, were ranged
   in columns before me,
When I was shown the charts and
   diagrams, to add, divide, and measure
   them,
When I sitting heard the astronomer where
   he lectured with much applause in the
   lecture-room,
How soon unaccountable I became tired
   and sick,
Till rising and gliding out I wander'd off by
   myself,
In the mystical moist night air, and from
   time to time,
Look'd up in perfect silence at the stars.

—WALT WHITMAN

Preludes

I

The lighting of lamps is a sign of hope in a bleak world.

The winter evening settles down
With smell of steaks in passageways.
Six o'clock.
The burnt-out ends of smoky days.
And now a gusty shower wraps
The grimy scraps
Of withered leaves about your feet
And newspapers from vacant lots;
The showers beat
On broken blinds and chimney pots,
And at the corner of the street
A lonely cab-horse steams and stamps.
And then the lighting of the lamps.

—T. S. ELIOT

Evolution: Philadelphia Zoo,
August 1987

So much is already over for the tortoise.
On the day we visit the zoo in crucifying
  heat,
he is a huge, dirty heart, all of his tires
  gone flat.
In the beginning, the animals must have
  had equal chances.

Think of the tiger practicing cunning while
  glaciers melted,
and the monkey tricking his way to
  questionable grace.
But the tortoise must have fumbled
  without a plan,
no engine of ambition throbbing under his
  hump.

No candle lighting the chambers of his
    brain,
and now look, he's a ruin in the dust. But
    no matter,
the zookeeper unlocks the gate and enters
    his yard
wearing her decent plain face and her
    coveralls,

dragging a hose to fill his small lake.
Even in the terrible heat, she is so serene
she might be a woman stepping into a
    bus
or handing a street vendor nickels for an
    orange,

and the tortoise slowly puts out his
    leathery head,
blinking his bald eyes. He can hardly
    believe
his luck. Trying to recall which leg to move
    first,
he starts out to greet her, full of clumsy
    joy.

When he finally reaches her, he butts his nose
against her thick thigh. She scratches his prehistoric
neck with her human fingers. There is no love
like theirs. Any minute they might begin

to sing. Any minute they might fly out of
their bodies like bright newfangled animals,
showing how veins and lovers and skeletons
can be perfected for something we never thought of.

—Jeanne Murray Walker

The Bat

Sometimes we think that reason can answer life's difficult questions. Yet often our hearts are mysteriously lifted and filled with hope, not by our own efforts, but by a sudden inner "wind change" described in scripture, and symbolized in the poem by the beating of wings that reminds the poet of the Holy Spirit.

I was reading about rationalism,
the kind of thing we do up north
in early winter, where the sun
leaves work for the day at 4:15.

Maybe the world *is* intelligible
to the rational mind;
and maybe we light lamps at dusk
for nothing . . .

Then I heard wings overhead.

The cats and I chased the bat
in circles—living room, kitchen,
pantry, kitchen, living room . . .
At every turn it evaded us

like the identity of the third person
in the Trinity: the one
who spoke through the prophets,
the one who astounded Mary
by suddenly coming near.

—JANE KENYON

The Room

With hope one can "praise darkness," know-
ing that new life is often born through pain.

Through that window—all else being
    extinct
Except itself and me—I saw the struggle
Of darkness against darkness. Within the
    room
It turned and turned, dived downward.
    Then I saw
How order might—if chaos wished—
    become:
And saw the darkness crush upon itself,
Contracting powerfully; it was as if
It killed itself: slowly: and with much pain.
Pain. The scene was pain, and nothing
    but pain.
What else, when chaos draws all forces
    inward
To shape a single leaf? . . .
        For the leaf came,
Alone and shining in the empty room;
After a while the twig shot downward from
    it;

And from the twig a bough; and then the
   trunk,
Massive and course; and last the one
   black root.
The black root cracked the walls. Boughs
   burst the window:
The great tree took possession.
                  Tree of trees!
Remember (when the time comes) how
   chaos died
To shape the shining leaf. Then turn, have
   courage,
Wrap arms and roots together, be
   convulsed
With grief, and bring back chaos out of
   shape.
I will be watching then, as I watch now.
I will praise darkness now, but then the
   leaf.

—CONRAD AIKEN

Untitled

Everything is plundered, betrayed, sold,
Death's great black wing scrapes the air,
Misery gnaws to the bone.
Why then do we not despair?

By day, from the surrounding woods,
cherries blow summer into town;
at night the deep transparent skies
glitter with new galaxies.

And the miraculous comes so close
to the ruined, dirty houses—
something not known to anyone at all,
but wild in our breast for centuries.

   —ANNA AKHMATOVA,
     translated by Stanley Hopkins Kunitz
     and Max Hayward

from *Prometheus Unbound*

In Greek mythology, Prometheus was the Titan[1] who stole fire from the gods and gave it to humans, along with all human arts and civilization. Here the poet describes virtues that will make the Titans "good, great and joyous."

To suffer woes which Hope thinks infinite;
To forgive wrongs darker than death or
   night;
   To defy Power, which seems
   omnipotent;
To love and bear; to hope till Hope creates
From its own wreck the thing it
   contemplates;
   Neither to change, nor falter, nor repent;
This, like thy glory, Titan, is to be
Good, great and joyous, beautiful and
   free;
This is alone Life, Joy, Empire, and
   Victory.

—PERCY BYSSHE SHELLEY

---

[1] The Titans were the offspring of Heaven and Earth.

March

The stormy March is come at last,
With wind, and cloud, and changing skies;
I hear the rushing of the blast
That through the snowy valley flies.

Ah, passing few are they who speak,
Wild, stormy month, in praise of thee;
Yet though thy winds are loud and bleak,
Thou art a welcome month to me.

For thou, to northern lands, again
The glad and glorious sun dost bring;
And thou has joined the gentle rain
And wear'st the gentle name of Spring.

Then sing aloud the gushing rills
In joy that they again are free,
And, brightly leaping down the hills,
Renew their journey to the sea.

Thou bring'st the hope of those calm
  skies,
And that soft time of sunny showers,
When the wide bloom, on earth that lies,
Seems of a brighter world than ours.

—WILLIAM CULLEN BRYANT

from *For the Time Being*

In times of distress, we need hope in the promises of God in order to continue trusting in God's goodness. This hope moves us forward into "Adventure, Art, and Peace."

Our Father, whose creative Will
Asked Being for us all,
Confirm it that Thy Primal Love
May weave in us the freedom of
The actually deficient on
The justly actual.

Though written by Thy children with
A smudged and crooked line,
The Word is ever legible,
Thy Meaning unequivocal,
And for Thy Goodness even sin
Is valid as a sign.

Inflict Thy promises with each
Occasion of distress,
That from our incoherence we
May learn to put our trust in Thee,
And brutal fact persuade us to
Adventure, Art, and Peace.

—W. H. AUDEN

from *An Essay on Man*

Hope humbly then; with trembling pinions[1]
    soar;
Wait the great teacher Death; and God
    adore.
What future bliss, He gives not thee to
    know,
But gives that Hope to be thy blessing
    now.
Hope springs eternal in the human breast:
Man never Is, but always To be blest:
The soul, uneasy and confined from home,
Rests and expatiates[2] in a life to come.

—ALEXANDER POPE

[1] A bird's wings
[2] To speak or write at length on a subject

Holy Sonnet XIV

Prayer itself is very often an exercise of hope. This famous poem is the poet's desperate acknowledgment that only God can rescue him from the prison of self. In his appeal, he recognizes that his only hope is that God will break the chains that bind him.

Batter my heart, three-person'd God; for
   you
As yet but knock, breathe, shine, and seek
   to mend;
That I may rise, and stand, o'erthrow me,
   and bend
Your force to break, blow, burn and make
   me new.
I, like an usurpt[1] town, to another due,
Labour to admit you, but oh, to no end,
Reason your viceroy[2] in me, me should
   defend,
But is captiv'd, and proves weak or
   untrue.

[1] Illegal seizure
[2] A governor ruling as a representative of a king or queen

Yet dearly I love you, and would be loved
  faine[3],
But am betroth'd unto your enemy:
Divorce me, untie, or break that knot
  again,
Take me to you, imprison me, for I
Except you enthrall me, never shall be
  free,
Nor ever chaste, except you ravish me.

    —JOHN DONNE

[3] Gladly loved

Scot's Form[1] in the Suburbs

The sedentary Presbyterians
awake, arose, and filed to tables spread
with white, to humble bits that showed
   how God
Almighty had decided to embrace
humanity, and why these clean, well-
   fed,
well-dressed suburbanites might need
   his grace.

      The pious cruel, the petty
         gossipers
      and callous climbers on the
         make, the wives
      with icy tongues and husbands
         with their hearts
      of stone, the ones who battle
         drink and do
      not always win, the power
         lawyers mute

[1] Holy Communion practiced in some Presbyterian churches in which believers sit at a table in the front of the church to receive the bread and wine commemorating Christ's death.

before this awful bar of mercy, boys
uncertain of themselves and girls
    not sure
of where they fit, the poor and rich
    hemmed in
alike by cash, physicians waiting to
be healed, two women side by side
    —the one
with unrequited longing for a child,
the other terrified by signs within
of life, the saintly weary weary in
pursuit of good, the academics (soft
and cosseted) who posture with
    their words,
the travelers coming home from
    chasing wealth
or power or wantonness, the
    mothers choked
by dual duties, parents nearly
    crushed
by children died or lost, and some
with cancer-ridden bodies, some
    with spikes
of pain in chest or back or knee or
    mind
or heart. They come O Christ, they
    come to you.

They came, they sat, they listened
    to the words,
"for you my body broken." Then
    they ate
and turned away—the spent
    unspent, the dead
recalled, a hint of color on the
    psychic
cheek—from tables groaning under
    weight
of tiny cups and little crumbs of
    bread.

    —MARK NOLL

While the Men Are Gone

In this imaginative poem, the poet sees life bursting forth all around her and her thoughts move into the great biblical vision of heaven and of the end of time where angels, elders, spirits, and living creatures fall down before the God of creation to worship and exalt Him.

All over Powelton Village, women are
    conceiving children
as though these were the last days before
    the Second Coming.
Sally Hammerman stands on the red brick
    walk beside
her fat twin, Rosie, & her thin twin,
    Phanny, reciting
the names of pregnant women, like a
    psalm

to destroy death. At Thirty-fifth & Baring,
someone's blond daughter waits for the
  bus, her stomach
lifting her flowered dress toward a second
  chance.
Before the bus can sigh & let her on, a
  woman raises
a 2nd storey window & cries for joy that
  she has conceived.

Nursling chrysanthemums on Marilyn
  Taylor's porch
open their purple eyes & praise the light.
We are all stocking children for nine
  months' delivery.
We are reveling in new bodies, we are
  filling
& emptying diaper pails, we are wiping
  noses,

we are never finishing our sentences, we
   are flying
apart, faces here, names there,
   occupation,
age address—our souls & bodies spinning
   quietly to pieces,
whirling closer & closer to the final light,
because this is the four horsemen & the
   four beasts

& the four and twenty elders[1] gathered
   around the sun.
Because the angel of birth has come to
   put one foot
on City Hall & one foot on the
   Wissahickon
& one foot on Baring Street.

—JEANNE MURRAY WALKER

[1] A reference to St. John's vision of the end of the world as recorded in Revelation

("Arcturus" Is His Other Name)

"Arcturus"[1] is his other name—
I'd rather call him "Star."
It's very mean of Science
To go and interfere!

I slew a worm the other day—
A "Savant" passing by
murmured "Resurgam"—
    "Centipede"!
"Oh Lord—How frail are we"!

I pull a flower from the woods—
A monster with a glass
Computes the stamens in a breath,
And has her in a "class"!

Whereas I took the Butterfly
Aforetime in my hat—
He sits erect in "Cabinets"—
The Clover bells forgot.

[1] The brightest star in the constellation Boötes

What once was "Heaven"
Is "*Zenith*" now—
Where I proposed to go
When Time's brief masquerade was done
Is mapped and charted too.

What if the poles should frisk about
And stand upon their heads!
I hope I'm ready for "the worst"—
Whatever prank betides!

Perhaps the "Kingdom of Heaven's"
 changed—
I hope the "Children" there
Won't be "new-fashioned" when I come—
And laugh at me—and stare—

I hope the Father in the skies
Will lift his little girl—
Old-fashioned—naughty—everything—
Over the stile of "Pearl."

—EMILY DICKINSON

Hope in the Bible

Why are you cast down, O my soul, and
why are you disquieted within me?
Hope in God for I shall again praise him,
my help and my God.

—Psalm 42:5,6

Happy are those whose help is the God of
Jacob, whose hope is in the Lord their
God, who made heaven and earth, the
sea, and all that is in them; who keeps
faith forever.

—Psalm 146:5,6

For surely I know the plans I have for you,
says the Lord, plans for your welfare
and not for harm, to give you a future
with hope.

—Jeremiah 29:11

For in hope we were saved. Now hope that is seen is not hope. For who hopes for what is seen? But if we hope for what we do not see, we wait for it with patience.

—Romans 8:24, 25

The Argument of His Book

I sing of brooks, of blossoms, birds and
  bowers;
Of April, May, of June and July-flowers.
I sing of maypoles, hock-carts[1], wassails[2],
  wakes,
Of bridegrooms, brides, and of their bridal
  cakes.
I write of youth, of love, and have access
By these to sing of cleanly wantonness.[3]
I sing of dews, of rains, and piece by
  piece
Of balm, of oil, of spice, and ambergris.[4]
I sing of times trans-shifting; and I write
How roses first came red and lilies white.
I write of groves, of twilights, and I sing
The court of Mab,[5] and the fairy king.
I write of hell; I sing and ever shall,
Of heaven, and hope to have it after all.

—ROBERT HERRICK

[1] Decorated carts that brought in the last of the harvest
[2] Toasts to someone's health at a festivity
[3] Wholesome lovemaking
[4] A substance used in perfumes
[5] The mischievous fairy queen who causes dreams

Seven Stanzas at Easter

Make no mistake: if He rose at all
it was as His body;
if the cells' dissolution did not reverse, the
    molecules
        reknit, the amino acids rekindle,
the Church will fall.

It was not as the flowers,
each soft Spring recurrent;
it was not as His Spirit in the mouths and
    fuddled
        eyes of the eleven apostles;
it was as His flesh: ours.

The same hinged thumbs and toes,
the same valved heart
that—pierced—died, withered, paused,
    and then
        regathered out of enduring Might
new strength to enclose.

Let us not mock God with metaphor,
analogy, sidestepping, transcendence;
making of the event a parable, a sign
   painted in the
         faded credulity of earlier ages:
let us walk through the door.

The stone is rolled back, not papier-
   mâché,
not a stone in a story,
but the vast rock of materiality that in the
   slow
         grinding of time will eclipse for each
   of us
the wide light of day.

And if we will have an angel at the tomb,
make it a real angel,
weighty with Max Planck's quanta, vivid
   with hair,
         opaque in the dawn light, robed in
   real linen
spun on a definite loom.

Let us not seek to make it less monstrous,
for our own convenience, our own sense
   of beauty,
lest, awakened in one unthinkable hour,
   we are
         embarrassed by the miracle,
and crushed by remonstrance.

   —JOHN UPDIKE

L O V E

WE OFTEN USE the word "love" lightly; we say, "I love chocolate," "I love your jacket," "I love tennis," when we mean we like something very much. We do use the word in one of its genuine meanings when we tell someone, "I love you." Romantic love, family love, love in friendship, different as they are, are rightly celebrated in songs, paintings, music, novels, and poems. The greatest of poets have written love poems that are masterpieces of literature. But the cardinal virtue, love, does not refer to romantic, nor friendship, nor family love in itself.

The older name for this last of the seven virtues is "charity." Today when we use the word charity, we refer to actions of giving that promote human welfare. Long ago, in the early days of Christianity, charity had a sublime meaning, far beyond the simple benevolence of helping others: in Christian thought, the supreme meaning of love is centered not in the frailty of human affection, but in God's love. Theologians teach that divine love fills all creation, and encircles every human being ever born. God loves us not because we deserve it, but because God *is* love. This assurance is found throughout the Bible, and most vividly in the gospels in the life, sacrificial death, and teachings of Jesus Christ. Jesus taught the disciples to call God, "Abba," meaning "Daddy," when they prayed. In Jesus' first-century Jewish culture, the father was the devoted provider and protector of his family. Using that image, Jesus wanted his listeners to view God as their loving, providing, protecting Father.

In Judaism, the love of God is incomplete without the love of fellow humans, which is expressed in relieving human misery, prejudice, and inequality. In the New Testament, the Greek word for this love is *agape,* signifying the highest form of love, which is giving of the self. *Agape* has its witness in the world: Mother Teresa's care for the poorest of the poor in Calcutta has become an international symbol of sacrificial love. But vast numbers of ordinary people, day by day, live their lives with quiet, unselfish love. Loving parents everywhere sacrifice for their children's well-being and expect nothing in return. People care for sick or handicapped relatives and friends. Married couples live lives of enduring devotion each to the other. People find it within themselves to love and forgive their enemies, to patiently love those who are broken, bitter, and angry. People serve others in disaster areas of the world, often in conditions of extreme personal hardship. Love, this greatest of the "theological" virtues, is expressed in committed, self-giving concern for others, in everyday small and sometimes heroic kindnesses, and in tender and generous acts.

Many poets have sensed the love of God in the universe. Certainly they write about romantic love, which can indeed be self-sacrificing. They also write about the benevolence that breaks through human doubts and troubles, that lifts the heart, and reaches out to others. Emily Dickinson catches the spirit of *agape* in her poem, "They Might Not Need Me—Yet They Might."

(They Might Not Need Me—
Yet They Might)

They might not need me—yet they
  might—
I'll let my Heart be just in sight—
A smile so small as mine might be
Precisely their necessity—

—EMILY DICKINSON

Love in the Bible

If I speak in the tongues of mortals and of
   angels, but do not have love, I am a
   noisy gong or a clanging cymbal.
And if I have prophetic powers, and
   understand all mysteries and all
   knowledge, and if I have all faith, so as
   to remove mountains, but do not have
   love, I am nothing.
If I give away all my possessions, and if I
   hand over my body so that I may boast,
   but do not have love, I gain nothing.
Love is patient; love is kind; love is not
   envious or boastful or arrogant or rude.
   It does not insist on its own way; it is
   not irritable or resentful; it does not
   rejoice in wrongdoing, but rejoices in the
   truth.
It bears all things, believes all things,
   hopes all things, endures all things.
Love never ends.

   —I Corinthians 13:1–8

To One, Now Gone, Who Always Let His Hunting Partner Claim a Downed Bird

I never knew he did not see
that sharing his own needs or pain
would be a showing of his trust,
not putting burdens off on us.
Nourished by his selflessness
we leaned on him too much and now
inexplicably have lost
what I thought we'd always have.
We never knew adversity,
except our own, to seam his face.
And now with every glimpse of human
  grace
he comes to mind, not welcome yet,
not with the ever-escorting grief.
There has to be a special place for him,
who held in more than he could bear
to shield the rest of us from care.
A rarity
who showed us what *agape* means.

—JIMMY CARTER

317

The Sweetest Lives

The sweetest lives are those to duty wed,
Whose deeds, both great and small,
Are close-knit strands of unbroken thread
Where love ennobles all.
The world may sound no trumpets, ring no
    bells;
The book of life the shining record tells.

The love shall chant its own beatitudes
After its own life working. A child's kiss
Set on thy sighing lips shall make thee
    glad;
A sick man helped by thee shall make
    thee strong;
Thou shalt be served thyself by every
    sense
Of service which thou renderest.

—Elizabeth Barrett Browning

Be Useful

Be useful where thou livest, that they may
Both want and wish thy pleasing presence
 still.
    —Find out men's wants and will,
And meet them there. All worldly joys go
 less
To the one joy of doing kindnesses.

 —GEORGE HERBERT

(I Had No Time To Hate)

I had no time to Hate—
Because
The Grave would hinder Me—
And Life was not so
Ample I
Could finish—Enmity—

Nor had I time to Love—
But since
Some Industry must be—
The little Toil of Love—
I thought
Be large enough for Me—

—EMILY DICKINSON

Baby

The tender love of parents for their children can be life's most self-giving love.

Where did you come from, baby dear?
Out of the everywhere into here.

Where did you get those eyes so blue?
Out of the sky as I came through.

What makes the light in them sparkle and
  spin?
Some of the starry spikes left in.

Where did you get that little tear?
I found it waiting when I got here.

What makes your forehead so smooth and
  high?
A soft hand stroked it as I went by.

What makes your cheek like a warm white
  rose?
I saw something better than any one
  knows.

Whence that three-cornered smile of
    bliss?
Three angels gave me at once a kiss.

Where did you get this pearly ear?
God spoke, and it came out to hear.

Where did you get those arms and hands?
Love made itself into bonds and bands.

Feet, whence did you come, you darling
    things?
From the same box as the cherubs'
    wings.

How did they all just come to you?
God thought about me, and so I grew.

But how did you come to us, you dear?
God thought about you, so I am here.

—George MacDonald

(If I Can Stop One Heart
from Breaking)

If I can stop one Heart from breaking
I shall not live in vain
If I can ease one Life the Aching
Or cool one Pain

Or help one fainting Robin
Unto his Nest again
I shall not live in Vain.

—EMILY DICKINSON

Love

Love bade me welcome; yet my soul drew
   back,
Guilty of dust and sin.
But quick-eyed Love, observing me grow
   slack
From my first entrance in,
Drew nearer to me, sweetly questioning
If I lacked any thing.

A guest, I answered, worthy to be here.
Love said, You shall be he.
I, the unkind, ungrateful: Ah, my dear,
I cannot look on thee.
Love took my hand and smiling did reply,
Who made the eyes but I?

Truth, Lord, but I have marred them; let
  my shame
Go where it doth deserve.
And know you not, says Love, who bore
  the blame?
My dear, then I will serve.
You must sit down, says Love, and taste
  my meat.
So I did sit and eat.

—George Herbert

But Not Forgotten

Whether or not I find the missing thing
it will always be
more than my thought of it.
Silver-heavy, somewhere it winks
in its own small privacy
playing
the waiting game with me.

And the real treasures do not vanish.
The precious loses no value
in the spending.
A piece of hope spins out
bright, along the dark, and is not
lost in space;
verity is a burning boomerang;
love is out orbiting and will
come home.

  —LUCI SHAW

Little Things

We need to ask forgiveness of the small and vulnerable creatures of our world for our human indifference to their suffering.

Little things, that run and quail[1],
And die in silence and despair!

Little things, that fight and fail,
And fall, on sea, and earth, and air!

All trapped and frightened little things,
The mouse, the coney[2], hear our prayer!

As we forgive those done to us,
—The lamb, the linnet[3], and the hare—

Forgive us all our trespasses,
Little creatures everywhere!

—JAMES STEPHENS

[1] Lose courage
[2] Rabbit
[3] Songbird

Winter Poem

once a snowflake fell
on my brow and I loved
it so much and I kissed
it and it was happy and called its cousins
and brothers and a web
of snow engulfed me then
I reached to love them all
and I squeezed them and they became
a spring rain and I stood perfectly
still and was a flower

—NIKKI GIOVANNI

(Who Has Not Found
the Heaven—Below)

Who has not found the Heaven—below—
Will fail of it above—
For Angels rent the House next ours,
Wherever we remove—

—EMILY DICKINSON

from *A Death in the Desert*

The essence of life and truth is to learn what real love is.

For life, with all its yields of joy and woe,
And hope and fear—believe the aged
    friend—
Is just our chance o' the prize of learning
    love,
How love might be, hath been indeed, and
    is;
And that we hold henceforth to the
    uttermost
Such prize despite the envy of the world,
And, having gained truth, keep truth: that
    is all.

    —ROBERT BROWNING

A Song of Love

Say, what is the spell, when her fledglings
   are cheeping,
That lures the bird home to her nest?
Or wakes the tired mother, whose infant is
   weeping,
To cuddle and croon it to rest?
What the magic that charms the glad
   babe in her arms,
Till it coos with the voice of a dove?
'Tis a secret, and so let us whisper it
   low—
And the name of the secret is Love!
        For I think it is Love,
        For I feel it is Love,
For I'm sure it is nothing but Love!

Say, whence is the voice that when anger
  is burning,
Bids the whirl of the tempest to cease?
That stirs the vexed soul with an aching—
  a yearning
For the brotherly hand-grip of peace?
Whence the music that fills all our being—
  that thrills
Around us, beneath, and above?
'Tis a secret: none knows how it comes,
  or it goes—
But the name of the secret is Love!
          For I think it is Love,
          For I feel it is Love,
For I'm sure it is nothing but Love!

Say, whose is the skill that paints valley
and hill,
Like a picture so fair to the sight?
That flecks the green meadow with
sunshine and shadow,
Till the little lambs leap with delight?
'Tis a secret untold to hearts cruel and
cold,
Though 'tis sung, by the angels above,
In notes that ring clear for the ears that
can hear—
And the name of the secret is Love!
For I think it is Love!
For I feel it is Love,
For I'm sure it is nothing but Love!

—LEWIS CARROLL

Cold Dawn at the Shelter

for Alva Steffler

Last Christmastide the angel came at six
fifteen. While volunteers began to poke
the guests awake, collect the mats, and
    fix
the coffee for the breakfast line, the
    smoke
rose from the first cigarettes, and one
    large man
groaned off the floor, breath harsh, a map
    of beet-
red lines high on his cheeks—he strains
    but can
not bend enough to reach his feet.

The angel teaches art design, his hair
is gray, he's fifty-odd. Straightway he
   goes
down on his knee, does not recoil from
   hot
dry skin, begins to tug one of a pair
of stained white socks around those
   death-puffed toes
and nonchalantly smiles and says "fear
   not."

—MARK NOLL

Sudden Light

I have been here before,
But when or how I cannot tell.
I know the grass beyond the door,
The sweet keen smell,
The sighing sound, the lights around the
    shore.

You have been mine before—
How long ago I may not know;
But just when at that swallow's soar
Your neck turned so,
Some veil did fall—I knew it all of yore.

Has this been thus before?
And shall not thus time's eddying flight
Still with our lives our love restore
In death's despite,
And day and night yield one delight once
    more?

    —DANTE GABRIEL ROSSETTI

"When All the World . . ."

A biblical Proverb (Proverbs 5:18) says, "May you rejoice in the wife of your youth." This poem reflects on the great blessing of lifelong love.

When all the world is young, lad,
And all the trees are green;
And every goose a swan, lad,
And every lass a queen;
The boy for boot and horse lad,
And round the world away:
Young blood must have its course, lad,
And every dog his day.

When all the world is old, lad,
And all the trees are brown;
And all the sport is stale, lad,
And all the wheels run down;
Creep home, and take your place there,
The spent and maimed among:
God grant you find one face there,
You loved when all was young.

—CHARLES KINGSLEY

from *Sonnet from the Portuguese*

This poem, written the year before the poet's marriage to Robert Browning, is one of the most celebrated love poems in the English language.

How do I love thee? Let me count the
    ways.
I love thee to the depth and breadth and
    height
My soul can reach, when feeling out of
    sight
For the ends of Being and Ideal Grace.
I love thee to the level of everyday's
Most quiet need, by sun and candlelight,
I love thee freely, as men strive for Right;
I love thee purely, as they turn from
    Praise.
I love thee with the passion put to use
In my old griefs, and with my childhood's
    faith.
I love thee with a love I seemed to lose
With my lost saints—I love thee with the
    breath,

Smiles, tears, of all my life—and if God
   choose,
I shall but love thee better after death.

—ELIZABETH BARRETT BROWNING

Love Over All

Time flies,
Suns rise,
And shadows fall.
Let time go by.
Love is forever over all.

—From an English sun dial

love is a place

love is a place
& through this place of
love
move
(with brightness of peace)
all places

yes is a world
& in this world of
yes live
(skillfully curled)
all worlds

—E E CUMMINGS

The Final Lesson

I have sought beauty through the dust of
   strife,
I have sought meaning for the ancient
   ache,
And music in the grinding wheels of life;
Long have I sought, and little found as yet
Beyond this truth: that Love alone can
   make
Earth beautiful, and life without regret!

—ARTHUR STRINGER

Song by an Old Shepherd

When silver snow decks Sylvio's[1] clothes
And jewel hangs at shepherd's nose,
We can abide life's pelting storm
That makes our limbs quake, if our hearts
   be warm.

Whilst Virtue is our walking-staff
And Truth a lantern to our path,
We can abide life's pelting storm
That makes our limbs quake, if our hearts
   be warm.

Blow, boisterous wind, stern winter frown,
Innocence is a winter's gown;
So clad, we'll abide life's pelting storm
That makes our limbs quake, if our hearts
   be warm.

   —WILLIAM BLAKE

[1] The forest

Putting in the Seed

Robert Frost so loved rural New England that he asked to be buried there. In this poem, the fertile earth in spring fills him with a sense of God's unending love and care for creation.

You come to fetch me from my work
    tonight
When supper's on the table, and we'll see
If I can leave off burying the white
Soft petals fallen from the apple tree
(Soft petals, yes, but not so barren quite,
Mingled with these, smooth bean and
    wrinkled pea;)
And go along with you ere you lose sight
Of what you came for and become like
    me,
Slave to a springtime passion for the
    earth.
How Love burns through the Putting in the
    Seed
On through the watching for that early
    birth
When, just as the soil tarnishes with weed

The sturdy seedling with arched body comes
Shouldering its way and shedding the earth crumbs.

—ROBERT FROST

Filling Station

*If the filling station stands for our fallen world,
the poem may direct our thoughts to God, the
"somebody" who brings order and beauty,
who "loves us all."*

Oh, but it is dirty!
—this little filling station,
oil-soaked, oil-permeated
to a disturbing over-all
black translucency.
Be careful with that match!

Father wears a dirty,
oil-soaked monkey suit
that cuts him under the arms,
and several quick and saucy
and greasy sons assist him
(it's a family filling station),
all quite thoroughly dirty.

Do they live in the station?
It has a cement porch
behind the pumps, and on it
a set of crushed and grease-
impregnated wickerwork;
on the wicker sofa
a dirty dog, quite comfy.

Some comic books provide
the only note of color—
of certain color. They lie
upon a big dim doily
draping a taboret[1]
(part of the set), beside
a big hirsute[2] begonia.

Why the extraneous plant?
Why, oh why, the taboret?
Why, oh why, the doily?
(Embroidered in daisy stitch
with marguerites,[3] I think,
and heavy with gray crochet).

[1] A low stool
[2] Hairy
[3] A plant resembling a daisy

Somebody embroidered the doily,
Somebody waters the plant,
or oils it, maybe. Somebody
arranges the rows of cans
so that they softly say:
ESSO—SO—SO—SO
to high-strung automobiles.
Somebody loves us all.

—ELIZABETH BISHOP

Good Deeds

If we do good deeds to benefit ourselves and not others, our acts then are not virtuous.

How far that little candle throws his
   beams!
So shines a good deed in a naughty
   world.

   —*Merchant of Venice,* Act 5, Scene 1

Heaven doth with us as we with torches
   do,
Not light them for themselves; for if our
   virtues
Did not go forth of us, 'twere all alike
As if we had them not.

   —*Measure for Measure,* Act 1, Scene 1

   —WILLIAM SHAKESPEARE

Abou Ben Adhem

Abou Ben Adhem (may his tribe increase!)
Awoke one night from a deep dream of
 peace,
And saw, within the moonlight in his room,
Making it rich, and like a lily in bloom,
An Angel writing in a book of gold:—
Exceeding peace had made Ben Adhem
 bold,
And to the Presence in the room he said,
"What writest thou?"—The Vision raised
 its head,
And with a look made of all sweet accord
Answered, "The names of those who love
 the Lord."
"And is mine one?" said Abou. "Nay, not
 so,"
Replied the Angel. Abou spoke more low,
But cheerily still, and said, "I pray thee,
 then,
Write me as one that loves his fellow
 men."

The Angel wrote and vanished. The next
   night
It came again with a great wakening light,
And showed the names whom love of
   God had blessed,
And, lo! Ben Adhem's name led all the
   rest.

   —LEIGH HUNT

A Devotional Sonnet

The poet expresses the modern dilemma of those who both "reject and want" God's love. In the end he affirms that even with his secular comforts and virtues, he belongs to God and God will keep him from straying too far from that love.

Lord, pity such sinners. Monday afternoon
Is not the proper time for Augustine.
My saints are porcelain, chipped clair de lune[1],
Books and white wine. But don't intervene:
My chastity, unwitting though it is,
Is Real; nor have I worshiped bitterness.
Jobless and on the loose, my share of bliss
Is simply that I've felt what I confess.

[1] The pale white or blue grey color which appears on the glaze of certain porcelains

And what absolves me? This chilled Char-
    donnay,
A few letters from Cambridge and Ver-
    mont,
And You, who will restrain me if I stray
Too far from love I both reject and want.
And should this be "interpreted disease,"
Yours are such sinners, such apologies.

   —TIMOTHY STEELE

Dear Land of All My Love

Long as thine art shall love true love,
Long as thy science truth shall know,
Long as thine eagle harms no dove,
Long as thy law by law shall grow,
Long as thy God is God above,
Thy brother every man below,
So long, dear land of all my love,
Thy name shall shine, thy fame shall glow.

—SIDNEY LANIER

Sonnet 116

Shakespeare asserts that if love is true, it never falters.

Let me not to the marriage of true minds
Admit impediments. Love is not love
Which alters when it alteration finds,
Or bends with the remover to remove.
O no! It is an ever-fixed mark,
That looks on tempest and is never shaken;
It is the star to every wand'ring bark[1],
Whose worth's unknown, although his
    height be taken[2].
Love's not Time's fool, though rosy lips
    and cheeks
Within his bending sickle's compass come;
Love alters not with his brief hours and
    weeks,
But bears it out even to the edge of doom.
    If this be error, and upon me prov'd,
    I never writ, nor no man ever lov'd.

—WILLIAM SHAKESPEARE

---

[1] A sailing vessel
[2] Only the ship can be seen, but not the value of the cargo.

Sonnet 29

When in disgrace with Fortune, and men's
    eyes,
I all alone beweep my outcast state,
And trouble deaf heaven with my
    bootless[1] cries,
And look upon myself and curse my fate,
Wishing me like to one more rich in hope,
Featur'd like him, like him with friends
    possess'd,
Desiring this man's art and that man's scope,
With what I most enjoy contented least;
Yet in these thoughts myself almost
    despising,
Haply[2] I think on thee, and then my state,
Like to the lark at break of day arising
From sullen earth, sings hymns at
    heaven's gate;
For thy sweet love rememb'red such
    wealth brings
That then I scorn to change my state with
    kings.

—WILLIAM SHAKESPEARE

[1] Useless
[2] Perhaps

The Last Invocation

At the last, tenderly,
From the walls of the powerful fortress'd
    house,
From the clasp of the knitted locks, from
    the keep of the well-closed doors,
Let me be wafted.

Let me glide noiselessly forth;
With the key of softness unlock the locks
    —with a whisper,
Set ope the doors, O soul.

Tenderly—be not impatient,
(Strong is your hold O mortal flesh,
Strong is your hold, O love.)

   —WALT WHITMAN

Not By Bread Alone

If thou of fortune be bereft,
And thou dost find but two loaves left
To thee—sell one, and with the dole
Buy hyacinths to feed thy soul.

But not alone does beauty bide
Where bloom and tint and fragrance hide;
The minstrel's melody may feed
Perhaps a more insistent need.

But even beauty, howe'er bent
To ear and eye, fails to content;
Only the heart, with love afire,
Can satisfy the soul's desire.

—JAMES TERRY WHITE

The Marriage of Heaven and Earth

Fire is a symbol of the love of God. In the opening stanza, a blaze in the fireplace melts the ice on winter windows. The fire then becomes a sign of renewal and morning in the poet's art, ending in a vision of a joyful dance of redemptive celebration.

Firelight in sunlight, silver-pale
Streaming with emerald, copper, sapphire
Ribbons and rivers, banners, fountains—
They rise, they run swiftly away.

Now apple logs[1] unlock their sunlight
In the many-windowed room to meet
New sunlight falling in silvered gold
Through the fern-ice forest of the glass
Whose tropic surface light may pierce
But not the eye. Oh, early world,
Still Daphne[2] of the stubborn wood
Singing Apollo's song in light;

[1] Logs from an apple tree, being used as firewood
[2] In Greek mythology, Daphne was a nymph loved by Apollo, but her father, a river god, turned her into a laurel tree. Apollo promised that the tree would be eternally green and took the laurel as his symbol.

Oh, pulsing constancies of flame
Warping a form along the log's
Slowly disintegrating face,
Crackled and etched, so quickly aged—
These are my mysteries to see
And say and celebrate with words
In orders until now reserved.

For light is in the language now,
Carbon and sullen diamond break
Out of the glossary[3] of earth
In holy signs and scintillations[4],
Release their fiery emblems to
Renewal's room and morning's room
Where sun and fire once again
Phase in the figure of the dance
From far beginnings here returned,
Leapt from the maze at the forest's heart,
Oh, moment when the lost is found!

—HOWARD NEMEROV

[3] A list of explanatory notes
[4] Flashes

The Great Lover

I have been so great a lover: filled my
  days
So proudly with the splendor of love's
  praise,
The pain, the calm, and the astonishment,
Desire illimitable, and still content,
And all dear names men use, to cheat
  despair,
For the perplexed and viewless streams
  that bear
Our hearts at random down the dark of
  life.
Now, ere the unthinking silence on that
  strike
Steals down, I would cheat drowsy Death
  so far,
My night shall be remembered for a star
That outshone all the suns of all men's
  days.
Shall I not crown them with immortal
  praise
Whom I have loved, who have given me,
  dared with me
High secrets, and in darkness knelt to see
the inerrable godhead of delight?

These have I loved:
        White plates and cups, clean-
    gleaming,
Ringed with blue lines, and feathery, faery
    dust;
Wet roofs beneath the lamp-light; the
    strong crust
Of friendly bread; and many-tasting food;
Rainbows; and the blue bitter smoke of
    wood;
And radiant raindrops couching on cool
    flowers;
And flowers themselves that sway through
    sunny hours
Dreaming of moths that drink them under
    the moon;
Then, the cool kindliness of sheets that
    soon
Smooth away trouble; and the rough male
    kiss
Of blankets; grainy wood; live hair that is
Shining and free; blue-massing clouds; the
    keen
Unpassioned beauty of a great machine;
The benison of hot water; furs to touch;
The good smell of old clothes; and other
    such—
The comfortable smell of friendly fingers,

Hair's fragrance, and the musty reek that
    lingers
About dead leaves and last year's ferns.

Dear names,
And thousand others throng to me! Royal
    flames;
Sweet water's dimpling laugh from tap or
    spring;
Holes in the ground; and voices that do
    sing;
Voices in laughter, too; and body's pain,
Soon turned to peace; and the deep
    panting train;
Firm sands; the little dulling edge of foam
That browns and dwindles as the wave
    goes home;
And washen stones, gay for an hour; the
    cold
Graveness of iron; moist black earthen
    mould;
Sleep; and high places; footprints in the
    dew;
And oaks; and brown horse-chestnuts,
    glossy-new—
And new-peeled sticks; and shining pools
    on grass—

All these have been my loves. And these
    shall pass,
Whatever passes not, in the great hour,
Nor all my passion, all my prayers, have
    power
To hold them with me through the gates of
    Death.
They'll play deserter, turn with the traitor's
    breath,
Break the high bond we made, and sell
    loves' trust
And sacramental covenant to the dust.
—Oh, never a doubt but, somewhere, I
    shall wake,
And give what's left of love again, and
    make
New friends, now strangers . . .

But the best I've known,
Stays here, and changes, breaks, grows
    old, is blown
About the winds of the world, and fades
    from brains
Of living men and dies.
Nothing remains.
O dear my loves, O faithless, once again
This one last gift I give: that after men

Shall know, and later lovers, far-removed,
Praise you: "All these were lovely"; say,
  "He loved."

—RUPERT BROOKE

Three Words of Strength

Schiller summarizes his vast learning in beautiful simplicity.

There are three lessons I would write,
Three words, as with a burning pen,
In tracings of eternal light,
Upon the hearts of men.

Have Hope. Though clouds environ round,
And gladness hides her face in scorn,
Put off the shadow from thy brow:
No night but hath its morn.

Have Faith. Where'er thy bark[1] is driven—
The calm's disport,[2] the tempest's mirth—
Know this: God rules the host of heaven,
The inhabitants of earth.

Have Love. Not love alone for one,
But man, as man thy brother call;
And scatter, like a circling sun,
Thy charities on all.

—FRIEDRICH VON SCHILLER

[1] Sailing ship
[2] Play

Directory of Poets

AKHMATOVA, ANNA, (1889–1966) b. in Ukraine. She is one of the two greatest women poets in the history of Russian poetry. Her first books, *Vecher* ("Evening") (1912) and *Chotki* ("Rosary") (1914), brought her critical acclaim. Her courage and incorruptibility during the Stalinist terrors, as well as her genius, have made her a heroic and timeless figure.

AIKEN, CONRAD, (1889–1973) b. in Savannah, Georgia. He was a fiction writer, critic, and poet, best known for the musical quality of his poetry. He won the Pulitzer Prize for Poetry for his *Selected Poems* (1929). He helped establish Emily Dickinson's reputation by editing and writing an introduction to her *Selected Poems* (1924).

AUDEN, W. H., (1907–1973) b. in England. He emigrated to the United States in 1939 and about the same time returned to the Anglicanism of his youth. He is one of the most important poets of the twentieth century with a startling style containing unusual meters, words, and images. His 1947 work *The Age of Anxiety* won the Pulitzer Prize.

BAUMGAERTNER, JILL PELÁEZ, (1947–) b. in Rapid City, South Dakota. She is an educator, literary critic, and poet. Her publications include *Flannery O'Connor, a Proper Scaring* (1988), *Poetry* (1990), and *Leaving Eden* (1995), a collection of her poems.

BAYLY, JOSEPH, (1920–1986) b. in Germantown, Pennsylvania. He was a journalist, editor, essayist, short story writer, novelist, and poet. His book of poems, *Psalms of My Life,* was published in 1971. He is well known for his satirical novels *The Gospel Blimp* (1960) and *I Saw Gooley Fly: and Other Stories* (1968).

BELLOC, HILAIRE, (1870–1953) b. in France. He was a historian, biographer, travel writer, novelist, and poet. He is best remembered today for his comic verse, *The Bad Child's Book of Beasts* (1896) and *Cautionary Tales* (1908).

BERRY, WENDELL, (1934–) b. in Port Royal, Kentucky. He is a novelist, essayist, educator, and poet. His poems have a quietly meditative air and are characterized by simplicity of line and a straightforward narrative structure. From his first collection, *The Broken Ground* (1964) to *Sabbaths* (1987), his poetry reveals a steadily growing concern with the abuse of the land and with the need to restore the balance of nature.

BISHOP, ELIZABETH, (1911–1979) b. in Worcester, Massachusetts. She was a writer and a poet, recognized as one of the best poets of her time. Her poetry is characterized by delicacy, wit, and keen intelligence. Her first book of poetry, *North and South,* appeared in 1946. She won the 1956 Pulitzer Prize for her second book of verse, *North and South —A Cold Spring* (1955). Her last book of poetry, *Geography III,* appeared in 1976. Posthumously published volumes include *The Complete Poems: 1927–1979* (1983) and *The Collected Prose* (1984).

BLAKE, WILLIAM, (1757–1827) b. in England. He was a visionary painter and poet, proclaiming the primacy of imagination and freedom over reason and law. Among the earliest of Blake's well-known poetic works are *Songs of Innocence* (1789) and *Songs of Experience* (1794).

BRONTË, CHARLOTTE, (1816–1855) b. in England. She first published poetry in a collection of poems by herself and her sisters Emily and Ann, under the pseudonyms Currer, Ellis and Acton Bell, in 1846. Her novel *Jane Eyre,* now ranked as a great English classic, was published in 1847 and brought her much success.

BRONTË, EMILY, (1818–1848) b. in England. Sister of Charlotte Brontë. In addition to her poetry, she wrote the masterpiece *Wuthering Heights,* which was published in 1847, a year before her death.

BROOKE, RUPERT, (1887–1915) b. in England. His poetry expresses the patriotism and romantic optimism of the early years of World War I. Handsome and talented, he became symbolic of youth wasted in war, when, following the disastrous expedition to Antwerp, he died of blood poisoning on his way to serve in the Dardanelles. His first volume, *Poems,* was published in 1911. His best-known work is the sonnet sequence *1914* (1915).

BROOKS, GWENDOLYN, (1917–) b. in Topeka, Kansas. Her poetry focuses on the conflicts of the everyday life of black Americans and the black community. She won a Pulitzer Prize for *Annie Allen* in 1950. Later works include *The Near-Johannesburg Boy, and Other Poems* (1986), *Blacks* (1987), *Winnie* (1988), and *Children Coming Home* (1991).

BROWNING, ELIZABETH BARRETT, (1806–1861) b. in England. She published her first volume of poetry, *An Essay on Mind, with Other Poems,* (1826) at the age of twenty. She was an established poet when she married Robert Browning in 1846. In 1850 her finest work, *Sonnets From the Portuguese,* was published.

BROWNING, ROBERT, (1812–1889) b. in England. Browning was one of the great Victorian poets. His abiding interests were the Italian scene, morality, and the complexity of the human personality. His collection of poetry, *The Ring and the Book* (1868–69), established his reputation as a major poet.

BRYANT, WILLIAM CULLEN, (1794–1878) b. in Cummington, Massachusetts. He was a lawyer, journalist, and the first significant American poet. His writings symbolize the romantic period's intense love of nature. One of his best-known poems, "To a Waterfowl," was written in 1815.

BUNYAN, JOHN, (1628–1688) b. in England. He was a fervent English Puritan best known for his allegory *Pilgrim's Progress* (Part I, 1678, Part II, 1684). He was imprisoned in 1660 for preaching without a license and spent the next twelve years in jail, where he produced nine books, including his spiritual autobiography, *Grace Abounding to the Chief of Sinners* (1666).

BURNS, ROBERT, (1759–1796) b. in Scotland. He is the best known of the Scottish poets, most admired for celebrating the simple earthy love between a man and a woman, the pleasures of drinking, and the fierce pride of the independent individual. His poems were published in 1786 in *Poems Chiefly in the Scottish Dialect.*

BYRON, LORD GEORGE GORDON, (1788–1824) b. in England. He was the most influential of the English Romantic poets. His epic-satire poem *Don Juan* (1819–1824), combining his storytelling gifts, his lyricism, and his unconventionality, is considered his masterpiece.

CARLYLE, THOMAS, (1795–1881) b. in Scotland. He was a social critic and historian whose writings pervasively shaped Victorian thought. His massive *Cromwell* (1845) was a powerful study of the possibilities of human greatness in history.

CARROLL, LEWIS (pen name of Charles Lutwidge Dodgson), (1832–1898) b. in England. He is famous as the writer of *Alice's Adventures in Wonderland* (1865) and *Through the Looking-Glass* (1872). His writing style is distinguished by humor and wit.

CARTER, JIMMY, (1924–) b. in Plains, Georgia. He was the thirty-ninth President of the United States. In his post-presidential years he has devoted himself to teaching at Emory University; diplomacy; the Carter Center, a research and advocacy center; and writing. His book *Always a Reckoning: And Other Poems* was published in 1994.

CUMMINGS, E. E., (1894–1962) b. in Cambridge, Massachusetts. He is widely known as a poet who was an innovative experimentalist. The spirit of New England dissent and Emersonian self-reliance underlies his verse, which is characterized by eccentric punctuation and phrasing. He was also an accomplished painter, playwright, and prose writer. His first book of verse was *Tulips and Chimneys* (1923). His twelve volumes of verse are collected in *Complete Poems* (1968).

DAVIES, W. H., (1871–1940) b. in Wales. His style is known for its force and simplicity, unusual for poets of his time. He stowed away on a ship to America where he took to the road, traveling through the United States, Canada, and other countries for thirty years, living the life of a recluse in spite of the popularity of his poems. His first volume of poetry was *The Soul's Destroyer, and Other Poems* (1905). His *Collected Poems* appeared posthumously in 1942.

DICKENS, CHARLES, (1812–1870) b. in England. He was a popular Victorian novelist, now regarded as one of the greatest English writers. As early as his novel *Oliver Twist,* (1837–

1839), his concern about modern society was evident. His most famous story, "A Christmas Carol," (1843) is an annual and traditional Christmas favorite and has made the name Ebenezer Scrooge a household metaphor for stinginess.

DICKINSON, EMILY, (1830–1886) b. in Amherst, Massachusetts. She is one of the finest poets of the nineteenth century, yet published only seven poems during her lifetime. Since her death she has been called the greatest woman poet since Sappho, who was born around 630 B.C. Her first volume of poems was published in 1890–1891, but a definitive edition did not appear until the mid-1950s when T. H. Johnson published her poems in 1955.

DONNE, JOHN, (1572–1631) b. in England. He was the most outstanding of the English metaphysical poets and a spellbinding preacher in the Anglican church. His poetry embraces a wide range of secular and religious subjects, including hymns and sonnets reflecting his own spiritual struggles, such as "A Hymn to God the Father" and "Batter My Heart Three-personed God."

DRYDEN, JOHN, (1631–1700) b. in England. He excelled in comedy, heroic tragedy, verse satire, translation, and literary criticism. He was poet laureate of England from 1668 to 1688 and wrote some of his best-known poetic satires during that time, among them, "Absalom and Achitophel" (1681) and "The Medal" (1682). Although he wrote essays and plays, he is known for his poetry's strength and polished elegance, and for his role as literary spokesperson for his generation.

DU MAURIER, GEORGE, (1834–1896) b. in France. He was an illustrator, cartoonist, novelist, and poet. Known chiefly for his novels that are concerned with love, friendship, and kindness, his novel *Peter Ibbetson* (1891) has become a minor classic, and has been adapted for the stage and cinema. His very successful *Trilby* (1894) pictures student life in the Latin Quarter of Paris.

EARHART, AMELIA, (1898–1937) b. in Atchison, Kansas. One of the most courageous women of her generation, Amelia Earhart made aviation history in 1932 as the first woman to make a solo flight over the Atlantic Ocean. In July 1937, as she attempted an around-the-world flight, her plane disappeared after takeoff from New Guinea.

ELIOT, GEORGE (pen name of Mary Ann Evans), (1819–1880) b. in England. She is one of the great realists of Victorian literature who developed the method of psychological analysis characteristic of modern fiction. *Adam Bede* (1859) was her first long novel and *Middlemarch,* written in 1871–1872, is her most admired and impressive work.

ELIOT, T. S., (1888–1965) b. in St. Louis, Missouri. He took up permanent residence in England in 1914 and became a British subject in 1927. He was a critic, playwright, editor, poet, and a leader in the modernist movement in poetry. He received wide recognition after the publication of *The Waste Land* in 1922. In 1948 he was awarded the Nobel Prize for Literature. *The Four Quartets* (1936–1942) were issued as a book in 1943 and are considered his masterpiece.

EMERSON, RALPH WALDO, (1803–1882) b. in Boston, Massachusetts. He was an essayist and lecturer as well as a poet. He valued self-reliance, optimism, universal unity, and the importance of individual moral insight. His book *Poems* was published in 1847.

FERLINGHETTI, LAWRENCE, (1919 or 1920–) b. in Yonkers, New York. He became associated with the beat movement of the 1950s. His first book of poems, *Pictures of the Gone World,* was published in 1955. His second work is his best known, *A Coney Island of the Mind* (1958). Selected poems were published in *Endless Love* (1981).

FRANKLIN, BENJAMIN, (1706–1790) b. in Boston, Massachusetts. He was a statesman, inventor, and writer, who made invaluable contributions to the Declaration of Independence and the U.S. Constitution. A man of prodigious energy and talent, he owned his own newspaper in Philadelphia in which he printed his popular and witty *Poor Richard's Almanack* (1732–1757).

FROST, ROBERT, (1874–1963) b. in San Francisco, California. He was one of the leading American poets of the twentieth century, and won the Pulitzer Prize four times. He had the remarkable ability to write poetry about nature that was deeply philosophical and unforgettably beautiful. His poetry collections include *Mountain Interval* (1916), *West-running Brook* (1928), *A Further Range* (1836), *Steeple Bush* (1947), and *In the Clearing* (1962).

GARRETT, GEORGE, (1929–) b. in Orlando, Florida. He is an educator, writer of short stories, screenplays, literary reviews, novels, and poems. His first collection of poems, *The Reverend Ghost,* appeared in 1957, and he has published numerous subsequent collections. A lifelong Episcopalian, he frequently draws on religious subjects for his poetry as exemplified in his poems "Revival" and "Buzzard."

GIBSON, WILFRID, (1878–1962) b. in England. He was a playwright and poet and became known in the 1920s and 1930s as "the poet of the inarticulate poor." His earliest works, *Stonefolds* and *On the Threshold* (both 1907), realistically portrayed the lives of English country folk. His later major works include *Coming and Going* (1938) and *The Outpost* (1944).

GIOVANNI, NIKKI, (1943–) b. in Knoxville, Tennessee. She is an educator, writer, lecturer, publisher, and poet. She has given numerous poetry readings and lectures at universities in the United States and Europe and is the recipient of many awards and honors, including honorary doctorates from several universities, including the University of Maryland, Indiana University, and Smith College. Her first book of poetry, *Black Feeling, Black Talk,* was published in 1968. Later collections include *Vacation Time: Poems for Children* (1980) and *Those Who Ride the Night Winds* (1983).

GLÜCK, LOUISE, (1943–) b. in New York, New York. She is a poet known for her insights into the self and her austere lyricism. Her first collection of poetry, *Firstborn,* was published in 1968. The poems in *The Triumph of Achilles* (1985) won the National Book Critics Award in 1985. Further works include *Ararat* (1990) and *The Wild Iris* (1992).

GOETHE, JOHANN WOLFGANG VON (1749–1832) b. in Germany. He is generally recognized as one of the greatest writers and thinkers of modern times. He is best known for his dramatic poem *Faust* (Part 1, 1808, Part 2, 1832).

GOLDSMITH, OLIVER, (1730–1774) b. in Ireland. He wrote prose, drama, and poetry. His most famous novel is *The Vicar of Wakefield* (1776) but he achieved his first success with his poem, "The Traveler" written in 1764. It praised English freedom but criticized the social evils of the time.

GOTTHEIL, RABBI GUSTAV, (1827–1903) b. in Poland. He lived in England before coming to the United States in 1873. He was a Reform rabbi and a Zionist leader. His book *Sun and Shield* (1896) is a collection of devout thoughts.

GRANT, JENNIFER (1967–) b. in Winfield, Illinois. She is a fiction writer and an award-winning poet. She has traveled extensively in Europe and Asia, and her poetry frequently draws from the people and places of her travels.

GUINICELLI, GUIDO, (c. 1230–c. 1276) b. in Italy. He studied law and was a judge in Bologna. His fame arises from the poem, "Of the Gentle Heart" but some twenty of his love poems survive. He is known as the most original poet of his time for giving truth and sincerity to love poetry.

HARDY, THOMAS, (1840–1928) b. in England. He was one of the most widely read English authors, producing fifteen novels, four collections of short stories, and eight collections of poems. His novels, including *The Return of the Native* (1878), *The Mayor of Casterbridge* (1886), and *Tess of the D'Urbervilles* (1891), established him as a master storyteller. In the last thirty years of his life he published about nine hundred poems that were generally concerned with what he saw as the human struggle against relentless and indifferent nature. Outstanding among his collections are *Satires of Circumstance* (1914), *Moments of Vision,* (1917), and, posthumously, *Winter Words* (1928).

HAYDEN, ROBERT, (1913–1980) b. in Detroit, Michigan. He was an educator and poet, whose subject matter was most often the black experience. His first collection was *Heart-Shape in the Dust* (1940). In 1976 he became the first African-American to be appointed poetry consultant to the Library of Congress. His later works include *Angle of Ascent: New and Selected Poems* (1975) and *American Journal* (1980).

HERBERT, GEORGE, (1593–1633) b. in Wales. He was an Anglican priest, dedicated to his parish duties, but who nonetheless was a writer and poet. His book *The Temple* (1633), is a superb collection of English religious poems, which includes almost every then-known form of song and poem.

HERFORD, OLIVER, (1863–1935) b. in England and emigrated to the United States when a child. For nearly forty years he worked as a writer and artist for magazines, including *Life* and *Harper's Weekly*. He wrote and illustrated fifty books of nonsense verse and poetry and was once known as "the most quoted man in America."

HERRICK, ROBERT, (1591–1674) b. in England. An English lyrical poet, he wrote more than 1,400 poems in his lifetime. Most of his poems were printed in *Hesperides* (1648). His greatest poem, "Corinna's Going A Maying" is a radiant invitation to love while it is still "springtime, fresh and green."

HOPKINS, GERARD MANLEY, (1844–1889) b. in England. He is a principal poet of nineteenth-century England although he published only a few poems during his lifetime. As a Jesuit, he served as a parish priest in England and later as a university professor in Dublin. His first collection, *Poems,* edited by Robert Bridges, did not appear in print until long after his death.

HUGHES, LANGSTON, (1902–1967) b. in Joplin, Missouri. He was a prolific playwright, essayist, fiction writer and poet, prominent in the Harlem Renaissance. His first book, *The Weary Blues,* was published in 1926. His poetic works include *First Book of Rhythms* (1954), *Selected Poems* (1959), and *The Best of Simple* (1961). *The Collected Poems of Langston Hughes* was published in 1994. His most enduring gift to literature was his belief in the commonality of all cultures and the universality of human suffering.

HUGO, VICTOR, (1802–1885) b. in France. He was the preeminent French literary figure of the nineteenth century. Although he is best known for two of his novels, *The Hunchback of Notre Dame* (1831) and *Les Miserables* (1862), he was also the most outstanding of the French lyric poets of his time.

HUNT, LEIGH, (1784–1859) b. in England. He was a very productive essayist, journalist and poet. He greatly influenced the Romantic Movement in English literature through his support of Coleridge, Keats and Shelley. His works include "Feast of the Poets" (1809), *The Story of Rimini,* (1816), and his poem, "Abou Ben Adhem" (1838). Hunt's *Autobiography* appeared in 1850.

JENNINGS, ELIZABETH, (1926–) b. in England. She established her literary reputation in the 1950s as part of an association called the Movement. Her work is quiet and unstrained and increasingly has turned to religious themes. Her first pamphlet, *Poems,* was published in 1953, followed by *A Way of Looking* (1955), both winning awards. Her *Collected Poems 1953–1985* appeared in 1986. She also has published poetry for children and a biography of Robert Frost.

JOHNSON, PAULINE (Tekahionwake), (1862–1913) b. on the Six Nations Indian Reserve, Brantford, Ontario, Canada. She was a Canadian Mohawk Indian who became a great literary and publishing success, reading her poetry throughout North America, and in London, England. "The Song My Paddle Sings" is one of her most quoted and inspiring poems. A collection of her complete poems, *Flint and Feather,* was first published in 1917.

JONSON, BEN, (1572–1637) b. in England. He was one of the outstanding English poets of the seventeenth century, and a great comic dramatist. His poetry chiefly consisted of satiric epigrams and verse epistles addressed to his friends and patrons. He is buried in Westminster Abbey in London under the inscription "O Rare Ben Jonson."

KEATS, JOHN, (1795–1821) b. in England. He was one of England's outstanding Romantic poets. Between the ages of eighteen and twenty-four he wrote poems that rank with the greatest in the English language. His first volume of poetry appeared in 1817 and included his famous poem "On First Looking Into Chapman's Homer." His poems of 1820, "Ode to a Nightingale," "Ode on a Grecian Urn," and "To Autumn," are unequaled for dignity, beauty, and imagery. He died of tuberculosis at the age of twenty-six.

KENYON, JANE, (1947–1995) b. in Ann Arbor, Michigan. Her first book of poems, *From Room to Room* was published in 1978. Her translation of *Twenty Poems* by Anna Akhmatova (1985) further established her reputation. Much of her poetry can be characterized by a sense of Christian humility and suggestions of God's mercy. *The Book of Quiet Hours* was published in 1986 and *Let Evening Come* in 1990.

KINGSLEY, CHARLES, (1819–1875) b. in England.

He was a writer, educator, social reformer, and Anglican clergyman. His popular *Water Babies* (1863) is a moralizing children's fantasy and his well-known *Westward Ho!* (1855) is a historical romance set in the days of Queen Elizabeth I, celebrating the days of seafaring explorers.

KIPLING, RUDYARD, (1865–1936) b. in India. He was educated in England and was the first English writer to win the Nobel Prize for Literature. Many of his works came from his experience of India. His collections of verse, including *Barrack Room Ballads* (1892), *The Seven Seas,* (1896), and *The Five Nations,* (1903) display a great range of subjects and style.

KUNITZ, STANLEY (1905–) b. in Worcester, Massachusetts. He is a scholar, critic, and poet who published his first book of poems, *Intellectual Things,* in 1930. He is known for his subtle craftsmanship and his treatment of complex themes. His *Selected Poems 1928–1958* won the Pulitzer Prize for Poetry in 1959. His later works include *The Poems of Stanley Kunitz 1928–1978* (1979) and *Next-to-Last Things* (1985).

LAMB, CHARLES (1775–1834) and MARY (1764–1847) b. in England. Together, the brother and sister wrote children's books, the best-known being *Tales from Shakespeare* (1807). Charles Lamb is best known for his *Essays of Elia* (1823, 1833) and for many essays on the works of Elizabethan dramatists. Mary Lamb's book, *Mary and Charles Lamb Poems Letters and Remains: Now First Collected with Reminiscences and Notes,* was published posthumously in 1874.

LAMPMAN, ARCHIBALD, (1861–1899) b. in Morpeth, Ontario, Canada. He was an important Canadian poet of the Confederation group who produced a remarkable number of poems during his relatively short life. His work is characterized by a sensitive recording of feelings evoked by the beautiful scenery of the Ontario countryside. He published *Among the Millet and Other Poems* in 1888 and *Lyrics of Earth* in 1893.

LANIER, SIDNEY, (1842–1881) b. in Macon, Georgia. He was a novelist, critic, musician, and poet. He fought in the Confederate Army and was captured and imprisoned in 1864. In 1867, a novel about his war experiences, *Tiger-Lilies,* was published, followed in 1880 by *The Science of English Verse.*

LARKIN, PHILIP, (1922–1985) b. in England. He was a novelist and highly regarded poet who in 1973 edited the *Oxford Book of Twentieth-Century English Verse.* His own poetry is seen to its greatest advantage in *The Whitsun Weddings* (1964) and *High Windows* (1974).

LAWRENCE, D. H. (1885–1930) b. in England. He was one of the outstanding British authors of the early twentieth century. In the course of twenty years, he published forty volumes of fiction, travel writing, social commentary, and poetry. Lawrence, with poetic vividness, attempted to describe subjective states of emotion, sensation, and intuition. His major novels include *The Rainbow* (1915), and *Women in Love* (1920). His poems were published posthumously in a collected edition in 1932.

LAZARUS, EMMA, (1849–1887) b. in New York, New York. She was a poet and essayist and is best known for her sonnet "The New Colossus" (1883), which is inscribed on a bronze plaque inside the base of the Statue of Liberty.

L'ENGLE, MADELEINE, (1912–) b. in New York, New York. She is a novelist, playwright, and poet, and is the recipient of numerous awards for her fiction. She published her first book of poetry, *Lines Scribbled on an Envelope and Other Poems,* in 1969. *The Weather of the Heart* (1978) and *Walking on*

Water: Reflections in Faith and Art (1980) followed subsequently.

LEVERTOV, DENISE, (1923–) b. in England. She moved to the United States in 1947 after publishing her first book of poetry *The Double Image* (1946). Her verse is deceptively matter-of-fact and reveals her concern with social issues. Important collections are *Candles in Babylon* (1982), *Breathing the Water* (1987), *A Door in the Hive* (1989), and *Evening Train* (1992).

LINCOLN, ABRAHAM, (1809–1865) b. in Kentucky. He was the sixteenth President of the United States and guided America through the Civil War. His eight volumes of writings, *Collected Works of Abraham Lincoln,* were edited by R. Basler and others, and published 1953–1955.

LINDSAY, VACHEL, (1879–1931) b. in Springfield, Illinois. His poems are studded with imagery and bold rhymes and express his patriotism and his romantic appreciation of nature. He first received recognition for the celebrated volume *General Booth Enters into Heaven and Other Poems* (1913). Subsequent works include *The Congo and Other Poems* (1914) and *The Chinese Nightingale and Other Poems* (1917).

LONGFELLOW, HENRY WADSWORTH, (1807–1882) b.

in Portland, Maine. He was the most popular American poet of the nineteenth century. His poem, "Evangeline" (1847) became the first enduring and successful long poem written in the United States.

LOWELL, JAMES RUSSELL, (1819–1891) b. in Cambridge, Massachusetts. He was a critic, essayist, editor, diplomat, and one of the finest New England poets of the nineteenth century. One of his most important pieces of writing was *The Vision of Sir Launfal* (1848), an enormously popular long poem extolling the brotherhood of man.

MACDONALD, GEORGE, (1824–1905) b. in Scotland. He was a prolific writer in a number of genres, including children's books, essays, poetry, and a total of twenty-six novels depicting Scottish life. He is remembered chiefly for his fairy stories of Christian allegory, best-known examples being *The Princess and the Goblin* (1872) and *The Light Princess* (1890). His classic children's book, *At the Back of the North Wind,* was published in 1871.

MAKEDA, QUEEN OF SHEBA, (c. 965 B.C.–925 B.C.). According to an ancient Abyssinian chronicle, the Queen of Sheba (modern-day Yemen) was famous for her beauty and wisdom. In the biblical account, I Kings, 10:1–

13, when she heard about the fame of King Solomon, she came to Jerusalem to test his wisdom.

MEYER, F. B., (1847–1929) b. in England. He was a pastor, conference speaker, teacher of Scripture, and one of the great biblical writers of his time. His devotional commentaries on books of the Bible are highly regarded classics.

MILOSZ, CZESLAW, (1911–) b. in Lithuania. He spent World War II in Warsaw, where he was active in the Polish resistance. He was a diplomat in the postwar Polish government, then lived in Paris before emigrating to the United States in 1960. Educated as a Roman Catholic, he became preoccupied with religious questions including the conflicting nature of moral and spiritual ideals. A novelist and social historian as well as poet, in 1980 he received the Nobel Prize for Literature and several of his works, such as *Selected Poems* (1973) and *Bells in Winter* (1978) were reissued.

MILTON, JOHN, (1608–1674) b. in England. He is one of the major figures of Western literature. His Christian epics, *Paradise Lost* (1667) and *Paradise Regained* (1671), ensure his status as the finest nondramatic poet of the modern era.

MOORE, MARIANNE, (1887–1972) b. in St. Louis, Missouri. She was a major American poet best known for her moral and intellectual insights and her witty ironic verse. Her first book, *Poems,* was published in 1921. Her *Collected Poems,* published in 1951, won the Pulitzer Prize, the National Book Award, and the Bollingen Award.

NEALE, JOHN MASON, (1793–1876) b. in Portland, Maine. He was a lawyer, novelist, journalist and poet whose early work included two narrative poems, "Battle of Niagara" and "Goldau," published in 1818. A flamboyant and enthusiastic writer, he produced many articles on American authors, edited a literary journal, wrote a religious treatise, *One Word More,* in 1854, and an autobiography in 1869.

NEMEROV, HOWARD, (1920–1991) b. in New York, New York. He was an educator, critic, novelist, and poet. His style is marked by irony and self-deprecatory wit. His books of poetry include *New and Selected Poems* (1960), *Inside the Onion* (1984), and *War Stories* (1987). In 1978 he received the Pulitzer Prize and the National Book Award for *The Collected Poems of Howard Nemerov* (1977).

NEWBOLT, SIR HENRY, (1862–1938) b. in England.

He is best remembered for his vigorous poems of the sea, including *Drake's Drum and Other Songs of the Sea* (1914). He was also a naval historian and wrote his autobiography *My World as in My Time* (1932).

NOLL, MARK, (1946–) b. in Iowa City, Iowa. Known chiefly as a historian, his first book, *Christians in the American Revolution* was published in 1977. Recent works are *A History of Christianity in the United States and Canada* (1992) and the award-winning *The Scandal of the Evangelical Mind* (1995).

NOUWEN, HENRI, (1932–1996) b. in The Netherlands. He was a Catholic priest, psychologist, educator, and acclaimed spiritual writer. He came to the United States in 1964, where his first book, *Intimacy,* was published in 1969. A recent work, *Life in the Beloved,* appeared in 1992.

PASTERNAK, BORIS, (1890–1960) b. in Russia. His novel, *Dr. Zhivago* (Eng. trans., 1958), helped win him the Nobel Prize for Literature in 1958. His first volume of poetry was published in 1913. In 1917 his second volume *Poverkh Baryerov* ("Over the Barriers"), established him as a major new lyric voice. His poems and some of his prose works have strong religious overtones. His lack of political interest was criticized by the Soviet government and for many years his verse was not allowed to appear in print in the U.S.S.R.

PATMORE, COVENTRY, (1823–1896) b. in England. His best poetry is in *The Unknown Eros and Other Odes* (1877), containing mystical odes of married and divine love, which he saw as a reflection of Christ's love for the soul. His ambitious novel in verse, *The Angel in the House* (in four books, 1854, 1856, 1860, 1863), exalts the sanctity of married love.

PATRICK, ST. (c. 389–461) b. in Roman Britain. He is the patron saint of Ireland, and was a bishop and missionary. At age sixteen he was sold into slavery in Ireland where he was converted to Christianity. He fled Ireland but returned in 432 as a bishop, determined to secure toleration for Christians and make converts. Although bitterly opposed by priests of the local religion, Patrick had great success. His feast day is March 17.

PAZ, OCTAVIO, (1914–) b. in Mexico. He is an essayist, literary critic, diplomat, and poet, and was one of the major literary figures in Latin America after World War II. In 1990 he won the Nobel Prize for Literature. His poetry explores the theme of the human ability to overcome solitude through love and art. Important verse collections include *Early Po-*

ems, 1935–1955 (1973) and *Collected Poems 1957–1987* (1987).

PINDAR OF THEBES, (c. 518 B.C.–438 B.C.) b. in Greece. He was the major lyric poet of ancient Greece, composing poetic songs for weddings, funerals, and religious festivals. What survives today are his *Odes,* written to celebrate athletic victories.

POPE, ALEXANDER, (1688–1744) b. in England. He is said to be the most accomplished verse satirist in the English language. At the height of his career, Pope addressed questions of religion and ethics in the didactic poem *An Essay on Man* (1733), for which he is most famous.

PUSHKIN, ALEKSANDR, (1799–1837) b. in Russia. Russians place him in the company of Dante, Shakespeare and Goethe as a towering figure in their literary heritage. Several of his major dramas recall great Russian heroes of the past, notably, *Boris Godunov* (1813) and *The Bronze Horseman* (1837).

RALEIGH, SIR WALTER, (c. 1552–1618) b. in England. He was a courier, military adventurer explorer and poet, and a favorite of Queen Elizabeth I. In the reign of James I he was accused of treason and sentenced to death. His most famous work is his unfinished *History of the World* (1614).

RATUSHINSKAYA, IRINA, (1954–) b. in Ukrainian S.S.R. She is a lyric poet, essayist, and novelist. In 1982, aged twenty-eight, she was arrested by the Soviet government as a political dissident and sentenced to seven years hard labor. She was released after serving four years in a labor camp. *Stikhi* ("Poems") (1984) was published in the West while she was still imprisoned. Other collections include *No I'm Not Afraid* (1986), *Beyond the Limit* (1987), *Pencil Letter* (1988), and *Dance with a Shadow* (1992). Currently she lives with her husband and twin sons in London.

RILKE, RAINER MARIA, (1875–1926) b. in the former Czechoslovakia. He is a foremost European poet of the twentieth century. His work expresses his search for objective lyric expression and, in later works, a mystical vision of the unity of life and death. One of his well-known books *Letters to a Young Poet,* was published posthumously in 1929.

ROETHKE, THEODORE, (1908–1963) b. in Saginaw, Michigan. His poetry is characterized by introspection and intense lyricism and his first book of poetry, *Open House* (1941), received acclaim. *The Waking Poems 1933–1953* (1953) was awarded a Pulitzer Prize. *Words for the Wind* (1957) won a National

Book Award and the Bollingen Prize. His *Collected Poems* was published in 1966.

ROSSETTI, CHRISTINA, (1830–1894) b. in England. Much of her poetry is religious; she was a devout member of the Church of England. Her first book, *Goblin Market,* (1862) displayed the strong lyric gift which characterizes much of her work.

ROSSETTI, DANTE GABRIEL, (1828–1892) b. in England. He was the brother of Christina Rossetti, and was a painter, designer, and poet. He won acclaim for his poem, "The Blessed Damozel" (1847) before he was twenty years old. Romantic love was the main theme in both his painting and poetry.

RUKEYSER, MURIEL, (1913–1980) b. in New York, New York. She is best known for her passionate concern with social issues and has a style of great flexibility, ranging from symbolic to lyric to satiric. A comprehensive selection of her earlier poetry is collected in *Waterlily Fire* (1962) and her *Collected Poems of Muriel Rukeyser* was published in 1978.

SASSOON, SIEGFRIED, (1886–1967) b. in England. He was a poet and novelist. As an officer in the First World War, he wrote poetry that expressed the brutality and waste of war. *The Old Huntsman* (1917) and *Counter-Attack*

(1918) were written in his typical forceful and realistic style.

SCHILLER, FREDRICH VON, (1759–1805) b. in Germany. He stands with Goethe at the forefront of German literature. He was a dramatist, philosopher, and historian, as well as a poet. Many of his dramatic ballads were produced in the years 1797 to 1799, including *The Song of the Bell,* 1799.

SENESH, HANNAH, (1921–1944) b. in Hungary. She is a national heroine of Israel, a poet and martyr. She left Europe for the safety of Palestine in 1939. In 1943, she volunteered for a mission with the British Army to help rescue Jews in her native Hungary. In 1944 she was captured, tortured, and executed by the Nazis at the age of twenty-three. A book of her poems, *Blessed Is the Match,* was published in 1947.

SHAKESPEARE, WILLIAM, (1564–1616) b. in England. He is the author of the most widely admired and influential body of literature ever written by one individual in Western history. His plays continue to be performed and made into films even today.

SHAW, LUCI, (1928–) b. in England. She came to the United States in 1953. Categorizing herself as a Christian poet, she is concerned with interpreting the world in symbols to involve the reader both in mind and heart. In addition to books of poetry, she has published a book on spiritual growth and on prayer. Her first book of poetry was *Listen to the Green* (1971). Several books of poetry followed, the most recent being *Polishing the Petoskey Stone* (1990).

SHELLEY, PERCY BYSSHE, (1792–1822) b. in England. He stands with Wordsworth, Keats, and Byron as one of the great English romantic poets. In the years 1816 to 1821 he wrote some of his most well-known poems: "Ode to the West Wind," "The Cloud," and "To a Skylark."

SMITH, STEVIE, (1902–1971) b. in England. She first came to prominence as the author of *Novel on Yellow Paper* (1936). Her first book of poems, *A Good Time Was Had by All* (1937), established her as a quirky, sardonic and entertaining poet. She produced several volumes of verse, including *Selected Poems* (1964).

SPENDER, SIR STEPHEN, (1909–1995) b. in England. His passionate and lyrical early verse was inspired by social protest against the abuses of the modern industrial world. In addition to poetry, he is a novelist, editor, and author of books of literary and social criticism. His autobiography, *World Within*

World, was written in 1951. He first attracted notice with *Poems* (1933) and *Vienna,* (1934). In 1983 he was knighted by Queen Elizabeth II.

STEELE, TIMOTHY, (1948–) b. in Burlington, Vermont. His work is collected in *Sapphics and Uncertainties Poems 1970–1986* (1995). His poetry has been called "classical," reflecting excellence in meter and technical rigor.

STEPHENS, JAMES, (1880?–1950) b. in Ireland. He was a poet and fiction writer best known for his fanciful and highly colorful prose writing. His first book of poetry, *Insurrection,* was published in 1909. The *Crock of Gold* (1912), with its rich Celtic theme, established his fame. In *Irish Fairy Tales* (1920), and *Deirdre* (1923) he made wide use of Irish legends and folklore.

STEVENSON, ROBERT LOUIS, (1850–1894) b. in Scotland. His children's adventure novels, including *Treasure Island* (1883), *Kidnapped* (1886) and his book of children's poems, *A Child's Garden of Verses* (1885) continue to be read and loved by today's boys and girls.

STRINGER, ARTHUR, (1874–1950) b. in Chatham, Ontario, Canada. He was a Canadian novelist, short story writer, screenwriter, dramatist, critic, biographer, and poet. His first book, *Watchers of the Twilight and Other*

Poems, was published in 1894. *The Woman in the Rain, and Other Poems* (1907) is considered one of his best collections.

TAGLIABUE, JOHN, (1923–) b. in Italy but has been a U.S. citizen all his life. He is a playwright, educator and poet. His first book of verse, *Poems, 1947–57,* was published in 1959. Further works include *A Japanese Journal* (1966), *The Doorless Door* (1970), and *Poems on the Winter's Tale* (1973).

TAGORE, RABINDRANATH, (1861–1941) b. in India. He won the Nobel Prize for Literature in 1913 for *Song of Offerings* (1910). The major theme of his prolific writings, including novels, songs, and essays, is humanity's search for God and truth.

TENNYSON, ALFRED, LORD, (1809–1892) b. in England. He was the preeminent English poet of his time. In 1850 he became poet laureate. One of his most important concerns was to combine social and state poetry with his own personal feelings and perceptions. He accepted a peerage from the British crown in 1884 to become Lord Tennyson.

TERESA OF ÁVILA, (1515–1582) b. in Spain. She is a principal saint of the Roman Catholic Church and a leading figure in the Catholic Reformation. One of the most remarkable women of all time, she combined intense practicality with rarefied spirituality. Her writings are considered literary masterpieces. One of her finest works, *Interior Castle,* was written in 1577.

THOMAS, DYLAN, (1914–1953) b. in Wales. He is noted for his highly original poems and his prose and plays. His most popular works include the radio play *Under Milk Wood* which was later adapted for the stage and posthumously published in 1954, and *A Child's Christmas in Wales* (1955). His *18 Poems* (1934) won him immediate fame. He is recognized as a major poet and his *Collected Poems* was published in 1953.

THOMAS, R. S., (1913–) b. in Wales. He is a Welsh poet with a central commitment to the Welsh language. His collection, *Song at the Year's Turning* (1955), established him as a poet concerned with the harsh realities of life in rural Wales. He was trained in theology and many of his poems reflect his exploration of life. One of his most recurring themes is "the meaning is in the waiting."

TURNER, STEVE, (1949–) b. in England. He is a biographer, journalist, and poet. His poetry books include *Nice and Nasty* (1980), *Up To Date* (1983), and *King of Twist* (1992). His most recent works are a biography of Jack Kerouac, *Angelheaded Hipster* (1996), and a book of poems for children, *The Day I Fell Down the Toilet* (1996).

UPDIKE, JOHN, (1932–) b. in Shillington, Pennsylvania. In addition to his many novels, for which he is famous, Updike has also achieved a reputation as a brilliant book reviewer and a poet. His favorite subject is middle-class manners, which he has examined from almost every possible perspective. In 1958 he collected his poems in *The Carpentered Hen,* and his work appears frequently in *The New Yorker* magazine.

VAN DYKE, HENRY, (1852–1933) b. in Germantown, Pennsylvania. He was a clergyman, educator, short story writer, and poet. Among his popular inspirational writings are the Christmas stories, "The Story of the Other Wise Man" (1896) and "The First Christmas Tree" (1897). His verse was collected in *Poems,* published in 1920.

WALKER, ALICE, (1944–) b. in Eatonville, Georgia. Her achievements as a writer are characterized by wide versatility. She is an essayist, biographer, novelist, and poet. Her novel *The Color Purple* (1982) won the Pulitzer Prize for Literature and was made into an acclaimed Hollywood film. Her published poetry collections include *Once* (1968), *Revolutionary Petunias* (1973), *Goodnight Willie*

Lee, See You in the Morning (1979), and *Horses Make a Landscape More Beautiful* (1984).

WALKER, JEANNE MURRAY, (1944–) b. in Parkers Prairie, Minnesota. She has been called "one of the best poets of her generation." She has won numerous awards and arts fellowships, including several from the Pennsylvania State Council on the Arts. Her first book was *Nailing up the Home Sweet Home* (1980). Her style is full of passion and wit, describing the commonplace and the bizarre with emotion and great dramatic power.

WASHINGTON, GEORGE, (1732–1799) b. in Virginia. He was commander in chief of the Continental Army during the American Revolution and the first President of the United States. His writings are collected in *Writings* (thirty-nine volumes, 1931–1944), edited by John C. Fitzpatrick.

WATTS, ISAAC, (1674–1791) b. in England. He was a minister, and has been called "the father of English hymnody." His several hundred hymns embody the stern doctrine of Calvinism, but are softened by gentleness and sympathy. His hymns include "Joy to the World," "When I Survey the Wondrous Cross," and "O God Our Help."

WESLEY, JOHN, (1703–1791) b. in England. He was the principal founder of the Methodist movement; a zealous reformer, he championed such causes as the abolition of slavery, civil rights, and prison reform.

WHITE, JAMES TERRY, (1913–) b. in Ireland. Art critic and lecturer, he is known chiefly for his biographical writings and works on the artistic heritage of Ireland. His book *John Butler Yeats and the Irish Renaissance,* was published in 1972.

WHITMAN, WALT, (1819–1882) b. in Long Island, New York. He was the greatest of nineteenth-century American poets. His book *Leaves of Grass* (1855) is one of the most inventive works of American literature. Whitman created a poetry that reflected the American melting pot of nationalities, the democratic hopes of the people, and the vastness of the United States.

WILDE, OSCAR, (1854–1900) b. in Ireland. He was an essayist, novelist, dramatist, and poet, known for his wit and brilliant theatrical comedies, notably *Lady Windermere's Fan* (1892) and *The Importance of Being Earnest* (1895). His poetry is reminiscent of Keats and Rossetti and he was known first in literary circles as a poet.

WILLIAMS, WILLIAM CARLOS, (1883–1963) b. in

Rutherford, New Jersey. He was one of the most innovative of American poets as well as a pediatrician who practiced medicine most of his life. He published more than forty volumes of poetry, fiction and plays. He was given, posthumously, the Pulitzer Prize in 1963 for his collection of poems, *Pictures from Brueghel* (1962).

WOJTYLA, KAROL (Pope John Paul II) (1920–) b. in Poland. The first collection of his poems in book form was published in 1979, a year after he was elected Pope. His poems from 1950 to the 1960s appeared in Polish Catholic periodicals under the pen names, Andrzej Jawien, and Gruda, the latter name a word that means a clod of the earth.

WORDSWORTH, WILLIAM, (1770–1850) b. in England. He was one of the earliest, and perhaps the greatest of English Romantic poets. His poems reflect his concern for the plight of workers displaced by the Industrial Revolution, and by England's wars, first with the American colonies and then with Napoleon. He was made poet laureate of England in 1843.

Acknowledgments

Grateful acknowledgment is made to the following for permission to reprint their copyrighted material. Every reasonable effort has been made to trace the ownership of all copyrighted material included in this volume. Any errors which may have occurred will be corrected in subsequent editions provided notification is sent to the publisher.

"The Room" from *Collected Poems,* Second Edition, by Conrad Aiken. Copyright © 1953, 1970 by Conrad Aiken. Reprinted by permission of Oxford University Press, Inc.

"Everything Is Plundered" from *Selected Poems* by Anna Akhmatova. Copyright © 1973, by Little, Brown and Company. Reprinted by permission of The Darhansoff & Verrill Literary Agency.

"For the Time Being" from *Collected Poems* by W. H. Auden. Copyright © 1976 by the Estate of W. H. Auden. Reprinted by permission of Random House Inc.

"What the Butcher Knows" by Jill Peláez

Index

422

424